Career Counseling
for People with Disabilit

Career Counseling
for People with Disabilities

*A Practical Guide
to Finding Employment*

· ·

Karen E. Wolffe

pro·ed
8700 Shoal Creek Boulevard
Austin, Texas 78757-6897

pro·ed

© 1997 by PRO-ED, Inc.
8700 Shoal Creek Boulevard
Austin, Texas 78757-6897

Library of Congress Cataloging-in-Publication Data

Wolffe, Karen E.
    Career counseling for people with disabilities / Karen E. Wolffe.
        p.   cm.
    Includes bibliographical references and index.
    ISBN 0-89079-722-6 (alk. paper)
    1. Vocational guidance for the handicapped—United States.
  2. Handicapped—Employment—United States.   I. Title.
HV1568.5.W65   1997
362.4′0484′0973—dc21   96-37178
                                                        CIP

This book is designed in Avant Garde and Goudy.

Production Manager: Alan Grimes
Production Coordinator: Karen Swain
Managing Editor: Tracy Sergo
Art Director: Thomas Barkley
Reprints Buyer: Alicia Woods
Editor: Debra Berman
Production Assistant: Claudette Landry
Editorial Assistant: Suzi Hunn

Printed in the United States of America

1 2 3 4 5 6 7 8 9 10   01 00 99 98 97

This book is dedicated in loving memory to my father, Harlan Douglas Wolffe, whose death on Labor Day in 1987 was apropos of his life—spent working to make our lives better. Thank you, Dad.

Love always, Karen

Contents

Preface

This book is intended to be used as a text in rehabilitation counseling, educational psychology, and special education courses. It could serve as the primary text in a rehabilitation course related to career counseling and job placement or a special education course on career education. In addition, it could serve as a supplemental text in an educational psychology course on career development and implementation. It should also prove helpful as a resource guide to counselors and educators who are practicing in public and private facilities. Finally, people with disabilities and their families are encouraged to use this book to guide relevant career planning efforts.

The book is divided into four major sections: Introductory Materials, Career Counseling Content Areas, Career Counseling for Clients with Differing Abilities, and Future Issues and Resources. The sections are subdivided into 14 chapters, as described briefly in this preface. Each chapter begins with a vignette, follows with content related to the concepts introduced in the vignette, and ends with application activities for the reader. The first five appendixes that follow the body of the text contain handouts related to each of the career counseling content areas: self-awareness, vocational selection, job seeking skills, job maintenance skills, and job search skills. Appendix F contains reproducible blackline masters of select figures that also appear in text.

SECTION 1: INTRODUCTORY MATERIALS

Chapter 1 introduces the reader to the area of career counseling and identifies potential clients. Clients are categorized according to their need for intervention, and this system is described in the first chapter. In Chapter 2, career development theories, including both structural and developmental theoretical constructs, are identified. In Chapter 3, the legislative history relevant to career counseling for people with disabilities is overviewed. Legislation particular to both education and rehabilitation is covered, including the Individuals with Disabilities Education Act of 1990, the Americans with Disabilities Act of 1990, the Rehabilitation Act of 1973, and the School-to-Work Opportunities Act of 1994. Chapter 4 presents information about using traditional vocational evaluation tools in career counseling and introduces readers to naturalistic assessment procedures.

SECTION 2: CAREER COUNSELING CONTENT AREAS

Specific counseling interventions are detailed in Chapters 5 through 9. Each chapter provides information and counseling techniques specific to a career development content area. The five content areas covered are self-awareness, vocational selection, job seeking skills, job maintenance skills, and job search skills. The self-awareness chapter includes information designed to help clients identify their interests, abilities, values, and liabilities, both from their own perspective and from the perspective of others. The vocational selection chapter covers exploring career options—what jobs are available that are related to clients' long-term career goals. The job seeking skills chapter encompasses the skills necessary to capture employment: the ability to locate job leads; to produce well-written applications, personal data sheets, résumés or qualifications briefs; and to interview successfully. The job maintenance chapter focuses on how to keep a job by understanding good work behaviors and employers' expectations, as well as how to evaluate and solve problems on the job. The job search chapter describes the application of the other areas: being able to successfully match one's self to jobs, identify prospective employers, produce and catalog paperwork required for employment, get out and meet with prospective employers, follow up on job interviews, and secure as well as maintain a job. Skills and behavioral competencies critical to each content area and ultimately to job placement are identified. Where feasible, I have provided worksheets and forms to facilitate in the counseling process.

Although it may seem a bit odd to have the chapter on job maintenance precede the chapter on job search strategies, it is essential that job seekers know what it takes to keep a job *before* they actually go out to get a job. Without job maintenance skills, job seekers are doomed to the "revolving door" syndrome—being able to find a job, but unable to keep a job. Therefore, I have included job maintenance content in Chapter 8 and job search techniques in Chapter 9.

SECTION 3: CAREER COUNSELING FOR CLIENTS WITH DIFFERING ABILITIES

Disability-specific considerations are covered in Chapters 10, 11, and 12. These three chapters are divided according to the categorical divisions introduced in Chapter 1: informational-level clients, instructional-level clients, and advocacy-level clients. These categories or client levels are based on the amount of intervention needed for success rather than traditional, medically based definitions of disabling conditions.

SECTION 4: FUTURE ISSUES AND RESOURCES

Chapter 13 delineates future trends in the provision of career counseling to people with disabilities. Topics covered in this chapter include self-determination issues, family involvement strategies, case management-for-life concerns, and the need for interagency coordination. In Chapter 14, the reader is introduced to local, state, and national resources in the fields of education and rehabilitation that may prove helpful in providing career counseling to individuals with disabilities. Following the text are helpful telephone numbers, a recommended readings list, and appendixes. The appendixes contain handouts and forms that can be used to facilitate learning in the major content areas covered in Section 2: self-awareness, vocational selection, job seeking skills, job maintenance skills, and job search skills. Appendix F contains reproducible blackline masters of select figures that also appear in text.

Learning activities are included at the end of each chapter. These activities are meant to give the reader an opportunity to apply what he or she has read in the chapter. I provide two approaches to enhancing the reader's knowledge in the area: reading activities and activities that involve doing things. Books that are mentioned for further reading are listed in the references. The learning activities are intended to be fun and easy to do.

Many thanks to the people in my life who helped make this book a reality. First and foremost, my heartfelt thanks to my parents, June and Harley Wolffe, who instilled in me a love for learning and an understanding of the importance of a work ethic to promote equality and self-esteem. To this day, my mother continues to help me in my office and with my life responsibilities and I appreciate her efforts. I also owe a debt of gratitude to my partner-in-life, my husband, Terry Hirsh, who tolerates the long hours at the computer and my frequent absences as I travel about the country sharing my perspective with individuals with disabilities as well as with other counseling and teaching professionals. He, too, helps me in innumerable ways with my life responsibilities. I thank my sister, Lisa, who opened her home and heart to me so that I would have a safe and quiet space to write when things became too hectic in Texas.

I owe an enormous thanks to Rick Roessler, who took time from his busy schedule to review my manuscript and give suggestions on how to improve it. My editor at PRO-ED, Jim Patton, deserves kudos, too, for his patience and guidance throughout the development of this project. I would also like to extend a formal thank you to Karen Thomas, my assistant, who works beside me daily. Finally, to the many friends and relatives not mentioned by name who have supported me throughout my career: Thank you!

I hope you will enjoy reading this book as much as I enjoyed producing it. If you have any questions or concerns about any of the material covered, please do not hesitate to contact me in care of PRO-ED, 8700 Shoal Creek Boulevard, Austin, TX 78757. I always welcome suggestions and whenever possible will incorporate your feedback into my work.

SECTION 1

Introductory
Materials

CHAPTER 1

Introduction to Career Counseling

Mandy wasn't sure what to do next. She had always tried to be as independent as possible. She had attended classes with her nondisabled peers throughout her academic career. She had gone to a good college in the Midwest and graduated from a liberal arts program with a major in English. She hadn't wanted a teaching credential, but now wondered if she should have followed her grandmother's advice to get one.

She had been born with spina bifida and had heard all her life how she couldn't do this and couldn't do that. The doctors had told her parents to commit her to an institution when she was born. They said she'd be retarded and never walk. The doctors had said she would be dependent on her parents all of her life. Well, she had been smart enough to graduate from college and she had learned to walk with standing crutches, but what now?

She'd tried unsuccessfully to find work since graduating 8 months ago. She had applied for jobs as a technical writer, a reporter, an editor, anything she could think of that was related to English. She wasn't even getting interviewed, much less employed! What should she do? Should she go to an employment agency and pay a fee for help? Would they assume, like so many other people without disabilities, that she couldn't work? Should she go to a rehabilitation agency even though she had avoided "special" services all her life? Could career counseling help her improve her situation? How? It seemed that most people either knew what they wanted to do and just did it or learned by trial and error. Of course, most people were not visibly disabled and didn't have to explain about crutches and braces. Ah well, it certainly couldn't hurt to go to the rehabilitation agency and find out about the career services they offered. At least there she wouldn't be the only disabled person applying.

CAREER COUNSELING

The primary purpose of this book is to explore career counseling techniques that have proven successful in helping people with disabilities help themselves make good life and career decisions. It is anticipated that public and private sector rehabilitation counselors, vocational guidance counselors, school counselors, and career counselors will be able to use the techniques included in this book in their work with young people and adults with disabilities. Specific objectives of this book include the following:

- Introducing counselors and educators to the need for comprehensive career counseling

- Broadening vocational guidance instructors' and school counselors' knowledge bases to include techniques for working with students with disabilities

- Broadening community-based career counselors' information bases to include techniques for working with adults with disabilities

- Providing a textbook-type resource to counseling and education students in higher education courses, who plan to work with individuals with disabilities

- Providing reference materials and suggested activities to practicing counselors and educators

Although career counseling is appropriate for people with or without disabilities, working with people with disabilities demands additional information on the counselor's part. It is critical that counselors have an understanding of the impact of disability on an individual's physical and emotional self. It is also important not to make assumptions about what a person can and cannot do based solely on information about disability. Counselors need to rely heavily upon information reported to them by their clients, particularly with regard to strengths and limitations imposed by disability.

Rehabilitation counselors and special educators typically assist individuals with disabilities in their career planning and job searches. However, not all students or adults with disabilities automatically seek or access such services. As described in the vignette, Mandy had neither participated in special education nor accessed rehabilitation services. Although this scenario is somewhat unusual for individuals such as Mandy who have congenital impairments, it is not without precedent. Typically, a counselor working with adults can anticipate that most individuals with disabilities will have participated in special education services or vocational rehabilitation services, depending on their ages and the onset of their disabilities. Regardless of whether an individual with a disability has participated in special education or rehabilitation services, a counselor cannot assume that a current or prospective client has received career counseling.

What Is Career Counseling?

A person's career is a combination of all the roles the person plays out over the course of his or her life (Brolin, 1993; Hoyt, 1975; Kokaska & Brolin, 1985; Super, 1976, 1980, 1990). A career includes the roles of child, student, volunteer, worker, community participant, parent, teacher, and mentor. Therefore, career counseling is about helping people determine what kinds of roles and jobs they would like to pursue over the course of their lives. Career counselors are facilitators. They help clients evaluate their strengths and weaknesses with both formal and informal assessment tools. They help people determine how they best match jobs in the areas in which they are interested and are best able to perform. Career counselors also help clients determine how to successfully search for and maintain employment. Counselors help clients analyze what job seeking techniques are working for them and help them correct techniques that are ineffective. They help clients stay focused and positive while working at finding employment.

Career counselors help their clients learn how to communicate effectively and develop good decision-making skills. They provide information to clients related to career and life planning resources, aids and appliances, related service providers, and community-based services. Counselors help their clients in any way they need assistance to be productive and feel good about themselves in their life roles.

Who Is Appropriate for Career Counseling?

Any individual can benefit from career counseling, if he or she is willing to invest time and energy in investigating career options for which he or she is best suited. Although youths and adults with disabilities can benefit from career counseling, their counselors need to be aware of disability-related issues and resources. Adults who seek out rehabilitation counselors typically do so of their own volition, although they may be encouraged by family, friends, or medical experts to seek assistance from these specialists. If a client is engaged in a counseling relationship for reasons other than personal growth or change, it is unlikely that the client will benefit. For example, if a client is attending counseling sessions only to please a parent or mate but doesn't really mind or is comfortable with being unemployed or underemployed, it is unlikely that a counselor or other service provider will be able to effect change. To bring about change, the individual must want to change, to improve his or her life.

How Does Career Counseling Effect Change?

Career counseling effects change by helping people analyze themselves and their opportunities to make good matches between the two. It empowers people who want to effect change in their lives to do so by teaching them self-advocacy skills and problem-solving strategies. With the development of problem-solving skills, they learn to set goals for themselves, both short-term and long-term goals. Self-advocacy skills or assertiveness skills enable people to present themselves well and interact with others in a nonjudgmental, productive way.

Career counseling provides individuals with information about themselves, the labor market, career options, good job matches, job seeking techniques, maintaining employment and interpersonal relationships, job accommodations, and so forth. With access to information, clients can make better decisions. Informed decision making is an important component of career counseling.

Where Does Career Counseling Occur?

Career counseling can occur in both individual and group settings. It can happen in schools, rehabilitation agencies, private counselors' offices, employment agencies, libraries, outplacement offices, or almost any other place where people congregate and discuss their future jobs, training, and life goals. Some people prefer to meet with a counselor on an individual, face-to-face basis. In fact, individual counseling is likely the most popular form of career counseling. However, many people have discovered the benefits of career counseling in a group. With a career counseling group, clients reap the advantages of individual attention coupled with the support of fellow job seekers. Group counseling can be particularly effective with disadvantaged or disabled populations of clients who tend to gain insights and encouragement from their peers as well as from the group facilitator. Azrin and Besalel (1980) detailed such a group approach for disadvantaged individuals in their book, the *Job Club Counselor's Manual*. Many of the techniques detailed in their book were redefined for people with disabilities in an applied learning lab, the Job Readiness Clinic, at The University of Texas at Austin from 1978 until 1991 (Daniels, 1978; Hansen, 1975; Wolffe, 1985, 1986).

CATEGORIZATION OF CLIENTS BY INTERVENTION NEEDS

Rather than encourage career counseling based solely on clients' physical, sensory, or cognitive impairments, this text differentiates among clients based on their needs for intervention. (Disability-specific resources, however, are included in the appendixes for counselor reference.) In the text, clients are distributed into three distinct groupings: informational, instructional, and advocacy. The following sections detail this categorization system.

Informational-Level Clients

Clients who fall into the informational category require a minimum amount of intervention. Typically, these clients are good readers and/or observers. In most instances, they can be given complicated or involved verbal and/or written instructions and be expected to follow through with directives received. In classroom settings, they can cope with traditional teaching styles (usually content-based lectures) and internalize information for future application. For informational-level clients, classroom-based learning activities are typically adequate for career definition and acquisition of job seeking skills.

If informational-level clients seek out services from rehabilitation counselors or community-based career counselors, they do so typically only for a brief period of time. They seek details from counselors about the labor market or insights concerning their job seeking skills, or they simply want to solicit leads. They may be newly disabled and need information about adaptive aids and appliances or compensatory techniques to do things they once did without assistance or adaptation. They take the information shared with them, generalize it, and apply it in their lives. They rarely return for additional services, unless they sustain injuries or must cope with chronic health impairments that require them to further investigate alternative skills or adaptive equipment for doing their jobs and/or they need to change careers.

Instructional-Level Clients

Instructional-level clients require an average amount of intervention. They don't assimilate information as quickly as the previously defined group, the informational-level clients. They learn best when they have the opportunity to "do" what they read and hear about in classes. This is known as process learning—that is, learning by doing activities with teachers or mentors providing input. Once these clients have mastered a concept, they can generalize and apply the content outside of the classroom context. Their school and community-based learning activities are sometimes sufficient for content mastery. However, they frequently apply for rehabilitation services following their school involvement for help with vocational decision making and mastering independent living demands. Their rehabilitation involvement is usually time limited. In other words, they may need financial help with postsecondary training or assistance with job finding only. Services provided are usually sufficient for achieving independence.

Instructional-level clients make up the bulk of the average career counselor's caseload. They need the counselor's guidance and insight to help them focus on what they can and would like to do, how to find job leads, how to successfully secure employment, and how to maintain employment. They may also need information and instruction in using adaptive technology on the job. Once services have been provided, however, instructional-level clients rarely need to return to the counselor. The exceptions are like those mentioned above: injury or chronic health impairment that causes job loss or potential difficulty on the job.

Advocacy-Level Clients

Clients who are considered advocacy level need extensive intervention, both in school and following graduation. Although they don't necessarily need assistance in all areas of their lives, they may need help throughout their lives in some areas. For example, one advocacy-level client may need assistance with money management or personal care but not job retention; another may need help only with transportation; and still another may need help with personal care, coaching on a job, supervised living, and most areas of life management. As a general rule, clients who have greater cognitive impairments need more assistance throughout their lives than those clients whose cognitive abilities are intact but who have multiple physical or sensory disabilities. The expectation is that advocacy-level clients will likely achieve independence in some areas of their lives while remaining semi-independent or dependent in other areas throughout their lives.

What many advocacy-level clients learn in schools and rehabilitation centers or workshops tends to be specific to the site and typically does not generalize to other places and situations. A community-based environment is often required for learning because generalization is difficult to achieve from a classroom environment or simulated work experience. With advocacy-level clients, learning in the milieu where they will be expected to perform (reflective of the next environment) is always preferable to learning away from that environment.

Although most people, with and without disabilities, tend to be informational, instructional, or advocacy level in most areas of their lives, the expectation is that no person performs at a particular level exclusively throughout his or her life. Often through study and practice, individuals can master skills and perform well in certain areas and they may be considered informational level in those areas. However, there are some areas where they simply don't have the interest or innate ability to perform at an informational level. For example, a person who has the ability to use his or her hands and basic tools to fashion items out of wood without guidance may be at the informational level in woodworking but at the instructional level or advocacy level in checkbook balancing. Likewise, an advocacy-level client who is unable to perform basic daily living skills or manage money may be able to play the piano and be considered informational or instructional level in piano playing. For a synopsis of the levels of intervention, see Figure 1.1.

All people can benefit from career counseling. Career counseling encourages individuals to identify their strengths and pursue life activities that promote their abilities. Career counseling for people with disabilities has only one difference, which is to identify factors imposed by physical, sensory, cognitive, or emotional limitations and develop compensatory skills or find adaptations to circumvent barriers.

. . . .

What Mandy did . . .

Mandy decided to find out what rehabilitation services might offer her. She met with a counselor, Mr. Watson, who suggested that she develop a plan with him of how the agency might help her. He explained to her that he could provide a vocational evaluation to help her identify her work-related strengths and weaknesses. He also said he could help with career counseling and guidance to help her better identify potential jobs. She thought it couldn't hurt to try.

The rehabilitation counselor and Mandy wrote a plan detailing what the rehabilitation agency could do to help immediately: provide a vocational evaluation and

---

Levels of Intervention

Informational-Level Client—Minimal assistance necessary

At this level, clients are good readers and observers. They can be given involved verbal directions and be expected to follow through with directives received. These clients cope fairly well with the traditional content approach to teaching. The teacher can lecture or lead discussions in topical areas and clients can apply what they have heard and seen. Clients learn by trying out new concepts in the environment and modifying them to suit their needs.

Instructional-Level Client—Average amount of help needed

At this level, clients are average performers. They can read and learn through observation, but demonstration is helpful. They can follow directions, but prefer to be shown and told how to perform. These clients respond best to process teaching. The teacher teaches by showing clients how to perform instead of assuming they will be able to apply what has been talked about or read outside of the classroom. Once a skill has been mastered, however, the client continues to refine and apply what has been learned in the community. With practice and training, it is anticipated that the majority of these clients will live independently and work competitively.

Advocacy-Level Client—Extensive support required, perhaps for life

At this level, clients function well below average in most areas of academics and daily living skills. These clients require intensive instruction, frequently one-to-one. Combinations of teaching methods will be necessary to get concepts across to clients. Instructions may need to be spoken, signed, written, pictorial, or other. Demonstration and coactive instruction may be most effective. Process learning is a must. Many clients at this level will be able to live and work in the community with supports, such as attendant care, communication specialists, job coaches, supervised living arrangements, and special transit.

Most people move between levels, depending upon the demands placed on them at any given time. However, people tend to function at or near one specific level most of the time. *Most clients, regardless of their need for intervention, learn best in environments where process learning is stressed.*

Figure 1.1. Levels of intervention.

career counseling. There was also a possibility for help with additional training, adaptive equipment or devices to facilitate employment, job leads and contacts in the community, or any other service deemed related to a vocational objective. She entered into a contract with the rehabilitation agency, known as an Individualized Written Rehabilitation Program (IWRP), which spelled out her responsibilities and the agency's commitment.

Before Mandy left Mr. Watson's office, they decided on a date for their first session. Mandy was pleased. It was great knowing that there was someone else out there working on helping her to find work. She wasn't alone!

Learning Activities

► **Reading**

Read Chapter 14 in Neff's (1985) book, *Work and Human Behavior,* and write a short report discussing your understanding of the social barriers to work discussed by the author. Detail your feelings and thoughts concerning the three fundamental ways he thinks a disability may handicap a worker.

Alternatively, read Bolles's (1991) monograph, *Job-Hunting Tips for the So-Called Handicapped or People who Have Disabilities,* and write a short review.

What do you think about his approach to addressing job seekers' and prospective employers' fears?

► **Doing**

Find out what kinds of career counseling services are available in your local community. Investigate by looking in the Yellow Pages of your telephone book; asking at a public library; checking with community colleges or universities; soliciting help through special education departments in public schools or through rehabilitation service agencies; and checking with private business and industry councils, state employment commissions, and the like. Develop a system for keeping up with the information you obtain, for example, a card file or database of names, addresses, and telephone numbers of local career counseling services. Then, do one of the following:

1. *Interview a local rehabilitation counselor.* Ask about the rehabilitation counselor's training, current job responsibilities, types of clients served, size of caseload, services offered, prior work experiences, and so forth.

2. *Interview a local school guidance counselor.* Ask about the school guidance counselor's training, current job responsibilities, types of students served, size of caseload, services offered, prior work experiences, and so forth.

Questions you may want to consider include these:

- Where does the counselor work? Would you be willing or interested in working in a similar location? Does the agency or school offer or pay for internships?

- What kind of a schedule does this counselor follow? Does the job require after-hours work and, if so, is there compensation time or overtime pay? Is there flexibility in terms of scheduling, in case you're using public transportation and have to match a bus or train schedule, or special transit services, or otherwise have to negotiate a ride? Are there people in the workforce who might be interested in carpooling?

- Are there day-care provisions?

- Where will you go for lunch?

- If you are a smoker, where will you smoke?

- If you are health conscious, where will you walk or jog or whatever before work, at lunch, or after work?

- If you have special needs, in terms of ramps or elevators, are your needs going to be met easily?

If you like, ask for permission from your interviewee, in advance, to tape-record your information interviews. If your interviewee feels uncomfortable with recording and refuses, you still need to write or otherwise record your observations for future reference following the interview. Note the positives and weaknesses for each job site you visit. Note specific information about the counselor you interview, for future reference. At a minimum, you will need name, title, address, phone number, and fax number or e-mail address, if applicable, in order to write a follow-up thank you note.

CHAPTER 2

Overview of Career Counseling Theories

When Mandy met with Mr. Watson, her counselor, he talked to her about different career counseling theories. He said the easiest way to think about career counseling theory was to divide the different theories into two major groups: structural and developmental. He said that theoretically a counselor could either look at a person's make-up or structure (what the person liked and was good at doing) and match that to different work environments or look at a person's level of maturity to see what job roles would be appropriate. Mandy wasn't sure she really understood.

Mr. Watson explained: Structural theories are sometimes referred to as trait–factor theories because counselors adhering to or following these theories encourage job seekers to look at themselves, identify their traits or personal characteristics, and then look at the work environment to see what factors are present that distinguish that job from all other jobs. Following an analysis of oneself and the workplace, a person determines whether or not there is a good match.

Developmental theorists, on the other hand, make the point that at different times in an individual's life the person will exhibit different personality traits as well as differing levels of skill. The developmental career theorists describe occupational choice as a process that evolves over time and may be irreversible. They believe that early influences, from family and experiences in childhood, influence a person's career choices. They suggest that clients receive counseling based on where they are in the developmental process.

Mr. Watson suggested to Mandy that for their purposes—trying to help her as an adult to determine a reasonable career choice—his inclination was to use a structural approach. Mandy was curious about what would be involved, so the counselor explained. He said that first he would have her take a pencil-and-paper test that would indicate her personality type. In fact, the test would provide her with a code, indicating the personality types she most resembled. She and her counselor would then look at the work environments where she would "fit" best. Mandy thought it sounded fascinating.

CAREER DEVELOPMENT THEORIES

Structural Theories

Structural theories are those that identify individual differences and attempt to analyze how personal characteristics or *structures* influence career choice. Structural theorists maintain that people have a limited number of personality characteristics and that these characteristics can be matched to appropriate work environments. Although a number of concerns related to the efficacy of using a structural approach exclusively have been raised since the 1950s, the theories described in this section continue to dominate the field of career counseling (Brown & Brooks, 1991, 1996; Osipow & Fitzgerald, 1996). In part, this is due to the fact that many people believe that a magical test will answer hard questions for them about their futures. However, the tests that have been developed by the advocates of structural theories are not in and of themselves a panacea for the hard work that career planning and career counseling involves; they are merely a component of the process.

One of the most influential people in the history of career counseling was Parsons, often referred to as the father of vocational guidance. In the early 1900s, he founded the Vocational Bureau in Boston, Massachusetts. He introduced the idea of matching individuals to jobs based on their "aptitudes, abilities, interests, ambitions, resources, limitations and their causes" (Parsons, 1909, p. 5). Parsons's vocational guidance model came to be known as the trait–factor approach because the counselor matched client attributes (traits) to workplace demands (factors). Parsons's trait–factor model dominated the field of vocational guidance through mid-century and is still used extensively in modern career counseling.

In contemporary career counseling, Holland is the primary structural theorist (National Occupational Information Coordinating Committee [NOICC], 1986). Holland's theory of vocational personalities and work environments details a system that categorizes people into personality types and identifies corresponding work environments for them (Holland, 1985). He identified six personality types and work environments: realistic, investigative, artistic, social, enterprising, and conventional.

Realistic people tend to want to work with things (objects, tools, and machines) rather than with other people or ideas. They are oriented to the present rather than to the past or future. Frequently, they are people with mechanical or technical abilities who like working in concrete, organized settings. Realistic types of people like jobs in agriculture, skilled trades, engineering, and the like.

Investigative people are analytical, abstract thinkers who prefer to work with their minds rather than their hands. They enjoy experimenting. They tend to be rational but original thinkers, and have interests in science, math, medicine, and technical areas.

Artistic individuals are perceptive, creative, free spirits. They rely on intuition and imagination. They think aesthetically rather than practically or concretely. They like unstructured environments. Artistic types gravitate to occupations in the performing and visual arts, as well as in other creative fields.

Social people tend to be gregarious. They like to be around other people. They are interested in people and like to help others. They typically have high verbal skills and enjoy careers in teaching, social work, counseling, and other helping professions.

Enterprising individuals are persuasive, assertive, and outgoing. They like to be in control and are often found in leadership roles. Enterprising people enjoy jobs in sales, politics, and business management.

Conventional people tend to be practical, neat, and well organized. They like structured, orderly environments. Conventional types do well in accounting, business, and clerical professions.

According to Holland, although each individual has a dominant personality type, few people are completely one personality type. Most people have personalities that fit into two or three categories. Holland has people rank order their personality types, using codes representing the types: R for realistic, I for investigative, A for artistic, S for social, E for enterprising, and C for conventional. He believes that the closer people can come to matching their personality types to work environments, the more satisfied they will be. Holland calls this phenomenon *congruence*. Incongruence occurs when individuals are placed in environments that are foreign to their personality types.

Holland also feels that some of the personality types are more consistent or compatible with one another than others. For example, realistic and conventional types have more in common than artistic and conventional types. Therefore, the realistic and conventional personality type will more easily find a comfortable placement than the artistic and conventional type. This concept, *consistency*, can be summed up as the degree of relatedness between personality types and environments. The more consistent an individual's personality type, the more predictable the person is likely to be.

Finally, Holland makes a third assumption about people and environments that he labels *differentiation*. What he has noted is that some people are clearly defined (their personalities are dominated by a single type), whereas other people have equal emphasis in all six types or some cluster of the types. The degree of definition is the individual's degree of differentiation. It is anticipated that highly differentiated people will have greater vocational and educational stability and satisfaction.

Developmental Theories

The developmental theories of career occupational choice began to emerge in the 1950s. They grew out of dissatisfaction with the seemingly "mechanical" aspect of trait–factor approaches. Some counselors felt uncomfortable with the notion of fitting people into slots based on their test results and an analysis of the work environments available. The developmentalists noticed that not all people approaching them for assistance were at the same level of readiness. Some of their clients were very immature in regard to work and others were quite sophisticated in terms of their knowledge of work and the opportunities available to them. The major developmental theories are described in the following sections.

Ginzberg, Ginsburg, Axelrad, and Herma (1951), one of the first groups of developmental theorists to present their ideas, postulated that occupational choice evolved as an individual grew up and was, for the most part, irreversible. They presented their theory of occupational choice as comprising three stages: a fantasy period, a tentative period, and a realistic period.

The *fantasy period* transpires over approximately the first 10 years of life. Children believe they can do whatever they want. They are engaged in active daydreaming about what they want to be when they grow up. Often their ideas about occupational choices are played out in role playing and fantasizing about various adult roles.

The *tentative period* encompasses adolescence, spanning the years between 11 and 17. In this time period, individuals test out their ideas about what they think they might like to do in the future. They hone their interests and abilities. The tentative stage incorporates the following subcategories: interests (11 to 12 years), capacity (13 to 14 years), values (15 to 16 years), and transition (17+ years). During the interests period, Ginzberg et al. assumed that children make their career decisions based on their highest interests. During the capacity period, youngsters begin to consider career decisions based on their abilities. Once individuals reach the values stage, their beliefs usurp their interests and abilities in career decision making. Finally, when they enter the transition to reality, at or about 17 years of age, they consider all three previous categories (interests, capacities, and values); however, their decisions are not yet reality based at this point.

The third and final period is the *realistic period*. As people mature and assume greater responsibilities, they implement their career plans. Exploration occurs as a consequence of making choices and reaping the rewards or coping with concerns that the decision elicits. When dreams meet reality, people make compromises. An individual's successful compromises lead to crystallization of a career path. Specification results when a career is defined and a final commitment is made. Although Ginzberg and his associates initially stated that the career choice process was irreversible and finite, they reconsidered their position. In the restatement of their theory, Ginzberg (1972) discussed career choice as a lifelong process that is largely dependent on decisions made early in life, but is not necessarily irreversible.

In the early 1950s, Super expanded Ginzberg's notions into his theory of career maturity, later reterned career adaptability, which he described as a cradle-to-grave evolution (Super, 1953). He summarized his theory in 1980 into his life-career rainbow, a graphic representation that presents the idea of multiple roles over one's lifespan (Super, 1980). The six life roles he identified that people will likely experience are child, student, leisurite, citizen, worker, and homemaker. Super wrote that vocational preferences and competencies that make up individuals' self-concepts change over time and with experience. The stages of development identified by Super are growth (birth to age 14), exploration (ages 15 to 24), establishment (ages 25 to 44), maintenance (ages 45 to 64), and decline (age 65 and beyond).

According to Super, during the growth stage, people develop their interests, abilities, aptitudes, and self-concept needs. During the exploratory stage, tentative plans are laid out and career choices are narrowed, but not necessarily finalized. During the establishment phase, people try out different job choices and ultimately settle on a particular choice based on work experiences. The maintenance stage occurs when a worker stabilizes in a job and puts energy into advancement and job improvement. During the final stage, decline, an experienced worker mentors younger people in the work environment and contemplates retirement.

The cognitive-behavioral theory builds on the work of the earlier theorists and superimposes the cognitive developmental models of Bandura, Ellis, Meichenbaum, and Skinner (NOICC, 1986). Perry (1970) defined the stages through which the cognitive-behaviorists believe individuals progress: dualism, multiplicity, relativism, and commitment.

Dualism, the initial stage, is characterized by individuals demonstrating simplistic thinking while relying on external forces for the bulk of their decision making. Dualistic thinkers cannot analyze and synthesize information well. They tend to see the world around them in "black and white," and to view things as either right or wrong. They also perceive jobs as either right or wrong for them, with little understanding of the complexities of the world of work.

Multiplicity follows dualism and occurs when people accept that there is more to decision making than simple either–or answers. Although individuals in this stage continue to have an external locus of control (relying on others for much of their decision making), they often recognize the need for decision making to occur as a process with their involvement. At this stage, they recognize, too, that career decision making requires consideration of multiple factors.

Relativism happens as an individual's locus of control shifts to an internal perspective. At this stage, people recognize that they are responsible for their own decision-making process. They begin to weigh the pros and cons of various occupational choices and visualize themselves in multiple roles over their lifetimes.

The final stage is *commitment* within relativism, during which an individual recognizes that an occupational choice narrows future decision making but also expands the boundaries of that life role. An individual's self-image and career identity become meshed. An individual's interests, abilities, values, and behaviors are consistent with one another.

No specific theory has proven more beneficial than others to people, with or without disabilities. Each counselor must choose the theory or combination of theories that most closely fits his or her own philosophical belief system and apply it in the counseling process. However, it is important to clarify that rehabilitation services are typically time limited. In other words, a rehabilitation counselor will have only a set amount of time in which to accomplish the goals set forth on the Individualized Written Rehabilitation Program (IWRP). Although the major theories covered in this chapter have all been successfully used by rehabilitation counselors providing career guidance to clients, rehabilitation counselors often choose structural theories over developmental theories due to time constraints.

. . . .

What Mandy did . . .

After Mandy and Mr. Watson discussed career counseling theory and decided to continue their work together, Mr. Watson gave Mandy a copy of the *Self-Directed Search* (SDS) to complete. The SDS was developed by Holland (1994) as a career counseling tool used to determine people's vocational personality types: realistic, investigative, artistic, social, enterprising, or conventional.

Mandy's CSE (conventional, social, enterprising) profile surprised her a bit. She had expected something more artistic after the discussion she and Mr. Watson had when she first approached him about this rehabilitation and career counseling process. However, when she looked up jobs in the *Dictionary of Holland Occupational Codes* (Gottfredson & Holland, 1989), she was pleasantly surprised to find jobs that appealed to her. She decided to investigate three further: caseworker, medical record technician, and catalog librarian.

Following her research and career counseling, Mandy decided to return to school for additional training in medical terminology and clerical skills. She completed the training on schedule and began looking for work. With a lead from her rehabilitation counselor, she found a job at a local military hospital as a medical records clerk. She was happy to find an entry-level job with good benefits, decent salary, and opportunity for advancement. In the future, her bachelor's degree would likely be an asset toward promotion. The present was a time to establish a track record. She felt very positively toward her coworkers and boss and was excited to be financially independent from her parents.

Learning Activities

▶ **Reading**

Choose one of the major theories discussed in this chapter and read articles, chapters, or books related to it. Write a short report detailing the additional information you are able to uncover. Be sure to include the pros and cons of using the theoretical model you have chosen with the kinds of students or clients with whom you are working or intend to work.

▶ **Doing**

Locate career counselors using the theory you chose above in their practices. Find out if one of the counselors would be willing to let you shadow him or her working with a client. (Understand that you will be held to strict confidentiality rules and be prepared to sign a statement to that effect.) Consider the following questions:

- How does the counselor implement theory into practice?

- Are there particular testing instruments that the counselor uses to determine where to start or stop with a client?

- Are the techniques the counselor uses appropriate for the setting in which you plan to serve (e.g., school or rehabilitation agency)?

- Does the career counselor you are observing work with individuals who are disabled? If so, does the counselor work with people with different kinds of disabilities or people with specific disabilities?

- If the counselor works with clients with disabilities, what kinds of modifications, if any, does he or she use?

CHAPTER 3

Legislative History

Brad was a graduate student in a rehabilitation counseling program. He was not new to rehabilitation. He had been working in the field for 3 years as a residential manager in a rehabilitation center that served people with head injuries. He had learned a great deal through the inservice training program at the center, especially about head injury. He had worked with lots of young men, some even younger than he, who had been involved in car, truck, motorcycle, and bicycle accidents. Many of the accidents had involved alcohol or carelessness—speeding, showing off, that sort of thing. It was enough to convince him to wear a helmet, even cycling in his own neighborhood.

He liked working at the rehabilitation center but he wanted to advance in his career. He felt he needed further credentialing; he hoped a master's degree would be the ticket. He thought he would enjoy the rehabilitation counselor position. He liked helping the guys figure out what they could be and how to go about making it happen.

The material he was having difficulty with in school was the history. What did he care where that legislative stuff came from and who said what? Was there any part of it that made sense to his work now and in the future? Could he pass the Introduction to Rehabilitation course this semester, without really understanding the importance of the history and legislation material?

THE HISTORY OF REHABILITATION

Prior to the 19th century, people with disabilities were considered as either damned or blessed and either disposed of or adulated accordingly throughout the world. The social and political movements that have affected people with disabilities in the United States since the mid-1800s include eugenics and Social Darwinism, the religious charities movement, the advent of compulsory education (followed by special education and vocational education), and, finally, rehabilitation.

By the mid–19th century, many states had laws based on the "science" of eugenics (which set forth the idea that mental deficiency and all other manner of disabling conditions, as well as pauperism and criminal behavior, were genetically transmitted) and Social Darwinism (which suggested that only the strong and fit should be allowed to survive). These laws prohibited the marriage of individuals with disabilities such as mental illness, epilepsy, mental retardation, alcoholism, or the like, and encouraged sterilization of such persons.

Simultaneously, religious charities were created to try to alleviate suffering among the disadvantaged and disabled. Unfortunately, in the beginning stages of the charity movement, it was assumed that poverty was a consequence of defects within an individual rather than misfortune. Gradually, however, the workers within the charities began to realize that, more often than personal defects, economic conditions were leading to dependency. Although this shift in thinking led to support for compulsory education and laid the foundation for adult rehabilitation services, the prevailing philosophy through the early and middle 20th century was one of segregated services for people with disabilities (Rubin & Roessler, 1995).

The most significant 20th-century legislation in rehabilitation and special education is described in the following subsections. These are followed by a section on current legislative initiatives pertinent to both rehabilitation and special education.

Rehabilitation

The first true vocational rehabilitation programs for people with disabilities were introduced at the end of World War I. Veterans with war-related injuries that presented a handicap to employment were provided with rehabilitation services by the Soldier's Rehabilitation Act of 1918 (P.L. 65-178). Its civilian counterpart, the federal Civilian Vocational Rehabilitation Act (P.L. 66-236), was passed in 1920. Although these programs for veterans and civilians were available in the 1920s and 1930s, they were poorly funded and considered as experimental. Therefore, many people in need of rehabilitation services were unable to receive them. A major breakthrough in rehabilitation legislation came about in 1935 with the passage of the Social Security Act (P.L. 74-271), which included a stipulation making vocational rehabilitation a permanent federal program (Wright, 1980).

The economic depression of the 1930s inhibited the growth of rehabilitation services. However, World War II and the advent of modern medicine, which saved the lives of many servicemen who previously would have died of their war-related injuries, prompted the expansion of rehabilitation programs. In addition, many civilians with disabilities were put to work in factories to provide munitions and other supplies to support the war effort. This surge in employment of people with disabilities afforded them the opportunity to demonstrate their abilities in the workplace. The Barden–LaFollette Act (P.L. 78-113), passed in 1943, extended federal–state rehabilitation services to include individuals with visual impairment, mental illness, and mental retardation. The act also expanded physical restoration services available to people with physical impairments (Moore & Fireison, 1995; Rubin & Roessler, 1995).

The 1950s and 1960s saw continued support for rehabilitation programs. Funding for client services and rehabilitation facilities increased. In addition, training opportunities for professionals expanded to meet the rehabilitation needs of people with disabilities. However, this momentum was stymied in the early 1970s when the nation's public policy of providing income maintenance to individuals with disabilities collided with the disability consumer movement. Mirroring the efforts of women and minorities, people with disabilities refused to accept separatism in their lives and began advocating for integration into the mainstream of society. The culmination of their efforts occurred with the passage of the Rehabilitation Act of 1973 (Public Law [P.L.] 93-112) and its subsequent amendments.

The Rehabilitation Act of 1973 was a landmark piece of legislation. Its amendments throughout the 1970s, 1980s, and 1990s strengthened it and specified what rehabilitation services would be like into the 21st century. The act removed the "vocational" component as the sole outcome for rehabilitation services and allowed rehabilitation personnel to work with individuals for whom the goal was independent living. By broadening the scope of outcome goals, the act provided for services to individuals with the most severe disabilities. It required client involvement in the rehabilitation planning process and introduced the Individualized Written Rehabilitation Program (IWRP) into the rehabilitation process.

The civil rights of people with disabilities are addressed specifically in Sections 501 through 504 of the Rehabilitation Act. Section 501 mandates nondiscrimination in the hiring of federal government employees. Section 502 addresses the issue of public accessibility by establishing the Architectural and Transportation Barriers Compliance Board to enforce accessibility promised in the 1968 Architectural Barriers Act. Section 503 mandates affirmative action by federal contract recipients. Any entity, including subcontractors, receiving more than $2,500 in annual federal contracts has to demonstrate nondiscrimination in employment and provide evidence of affirmative action efforts.

The backbone of civil rights legislation for people with disabilities is Section 504 of the Rehabilitation Act of 1973. Section 504 prohibits the exclusion of people with disabilities (who are otherwise qualified) from participation in any program or activity receiving federal financial assistance, including social institutions such as colleges and universities, day-care centers, hospitals, and the like. The legal protection provided to people with disabilities under Section 504 is another important element contained in the Rehabilitation Act of 1973 (Rubin & Roessler, 1995; Stafford, 1995).

Special Education

Specialized educational programming for children with disabilities parallels rehabilitation efforts with disabled adults. Although there was a smattering of efforts to educate children with special needs in the 18th century, including Itard's work with children who were deaf (Patton, Kauffman, Blackbourn, & Brown, 1991) and Hauy's work with children who were blind (Koestler, 1976; Lowenfeld, 1973), it was not until the 19th century that systematic education of students with disabilities became the norm. However, it should be noted that, for the most part, these early efforts to educate children with disabilities occurred in segregated environments. Special schools for children who were blind, deaf, or mentally retarded were established throughout the United States. In only a few locations, children with special needs were welcomed into day school programs with their nondisabled peers.

The education of children with special needs, like the rehabilitation effort, was negatively influenced in the early part of the 19th century by the eugenics movement. However, following World War II and the Korean War and the integration of war-wounded into mainstream society, people's attitudes toward individuals with disabilities once again changed and became more favorable. By 1948, the majority of states mandated some special education services be provided in the local schools. Services expanded throughout the 1950s and 1960s, culminating with legislative action in the Elementary and Secondary Education Act of 1965 which included service delivery to children with disabilities. Amendments to this act during the late 1960s continued to expand special education services and created the Bureau of Education for the Handicapped, the precursor to the Office of Special Education Programs (Patton et al., 1991).

Landmark special education legislation, P.L. 94-142, the Education of All Handicapped Children Act, was enacted in 1975. This act guaranteed a free, appropriate education in the least restrictive environment for all children with disabilities. This legislation was amended in 1983 (P.L. 98-199) to provide transition initiatives and in 1986 (P.L. 99-457) to allow for services to infants, toddlers, preschoolers, and their families. In the 1990 amendments, the act was renamed the Individuals with Disabilities Education Act (IDEA) and given a new public law number, P.L. 101-476. IDEA expands the authority of private citizens and authorizes them to sue states or departments of education for violations of IDEA. The law also includes a definition of transition services and mandates that transition services be addressed in the IEP of each student in special education by age 16 or earlier, if appropriate (Wehman, 1992).

CURRENT LEGISLATIVE INITIATIVES

Rehabilitation Initiatives

Rehabilitation Act Amendments

Significant amendments were made to the Rehabilitation Act of 1973 in 1986 and in 1992. The 1986 amendments (P.L. 99-506) focused on the need for access to technology and increasing employability, particularly of individuals with severe disabilities. Rehabilitation engineering services were expanded and rehabilitation agencies were encouraged to develop collaborative agreements with other public entities and nonprofit organizations providing vocational skills training employment services to individuals with severe disabilities. Supported employment services also were authorized in the 1986 amendments.

The Rehabilitation Act Amendments of 1992 (P.L. 102-569) contain the most sweeping changes to the Rehabilitation Act since it was passed in 1973 (Stafford, 1995). However, in many respects the intent of the law is consistent: to provide services to the most severely disabled, to guarantee rights and remedies to people with disabilities, and to expand the input and choice of individuals with disabilities. States are required to define who the most severely disabled are and give them priority in the delivery of services. In addition, only the most severely disabled are eligible for supported employment assistance. For the first time, the act contains an employment outcome definition, emphasizing full- or part-time work in the integrated labor market. Another significant change is the requirement that eligibility be determined within 60 days of receipt of a client's application. The major focal point throughout the act is on integration of individuals with disabilities.

The current Rehabilitation Act, as amended, expires in 1997. The following are some issues that will be considered in the reauthorization process:

- The impact of workforce development and job training consolidation legislation that Congress passed in 1995

- Federal government efforts to streamline bureaucratic requirements, consolidate funding streams, and shift responsibility for government services to the local level

- Increased client involvement and better operationalization of consumer choice in rehabilitation programs

Americans with Disabilities Act

With the passage of P.L. 101-336, the Americans with Disabilities Act (ADA) of 1990, employment opportunities are expected to expand for individuals with disabilities. Advocates for people with disabilities hope this piece of legislation will truly bring people with disabilities into the mainstream of society, thereby combating negative stereotypes. Title I of the ADA addresses employment issues specifically. (As of July 26, 1992, employers with 25 or more employees were covered by the ADA. Likewise, as of July 26, 1994, employers with 15 or more employees were covered by the ADA.) Provisions in Title I include the following:

- Employers, employment agencies, labor unions, or joint labor–management committees are prohibited from discriminating against a qualified person with a disability in the job application process, hiring decisions, advancement, employment termination, compensation, training, or other employment conditions.

- Employers are required to make reasonable accommodations of known physical or mental limitations for a qualified person with a disability, unless doing so would impose undue hardship on the employer.

- Use of employment tests, qualification standards, or selection criteria intended to screen out applicants with disabilities is prohibited.

In addition to its employment-related provisions, the ADA contains provisions in four additional areas that will help to combat negative stereotyping of people with disabilities. Title II, which is concerned with *public services*, covers two major areas: accessibility to public services, programs, or activities, and access to transportation. Title III prohibits discrimination against people with disabilities in *public accommodations*, including full and equal enjoyment of services, goods, facilities, privileges, or accommodations in places used by the general public for employment, travel, trade, transportation, communication, or entertainment. Title IV, involving *telecommunications*, requires local and regional telephone companies to provide telecommunication relay services. It also requires closed captioning of public service announcements produced with federal money. Finally, Title V contains *miscellaneous* provisions that describe ADA's relationship to other laws, including amendments to the Rehabilitation Act of 1973. Title V also explains insurance issues, prohibits state immunity, prohibits retaliation or coercion against employees, sets regulations and timetables for ADA implementation, provides for recovering attorney's fees, and describes ADA coverage to Congress and agencies of the legislative branch.

Special Education Initiatives

Reauthorization of IDEA

In spite of months of negotiations, the U.S. Congress adjourned in the fall of 1996 without reauthorizing the Individuals with Disabilities Education Act (IDEA). Although it is anticipated that the act will be reauthorized in 1997, there are serious disagreements still to be worked out between disability organizations, teacher and administrator groups, and U.S. representatives and senators. Some of the more controversial amendments that elicited the stalemate are discipline procedures for students with disabilities who demonstrate disruptive or violent behaviors in school, including elimination of a school district's responsibility to provide educational services to expelled special education students; changes to the federal funding formula that provides money to states based on the number of students in public school rather than a head count of eligible students as the current formula allows; curtailing the awarding of fees to families' attorneys in some situations; and exceptions to personnel requirements in areas where there are personnel shortages (Brady, 1996).

School-to-Work Opportunities Act

In 1994, the U.S. Congress passed the School-to-Work Opportunities Act (P.L. 103-239) in an effort to make learning more meaningful for all students. The key to the new approach is to structure the learning environment toward students' future careers in the belief that students learn best when they apply what they learn in classrooms to real life and work situations. There are three core elements to the school-to-work system:

- School-based learning activities that are based on high academic and business-defined vocational skills standards

- Work-based learning activities such as career exploration and work experiences

- Connecting activities that integrate classroom and on-the-job skills instruction

The movement in education toward outcome-based learning lends itself to increased efforts by career counselors to work with students with disabilities during their academic involvement. Likewise, the renewed emphasis in rehabilitation on providing transition services to youth with disabilities, in addition to services for adults, underscores the need for career counseling throughout the rehabilitation system as well.

Learning Activities

▶ Reading

Read about the *history of rehabilitation* in Rubin and Roessler's (1995) *Foundations of the Vocational Rehabilitation Process* or Parker and Syzmanski's (1992) *Rehabilitation Counseling: Basics and Beyond.* Or read about the *history of special education* in *Exceptional Children in Focus* by Patton, Kauffman, Blackbourn, and Brown (1991) and/or career education in Brolin's (1993) *Life Centered Career Education,* Kokaska and Brolin's (1985) *Career Education for Individuals with Disabilities,* or Clark's (1990) *Career Development and Transition Education for Adolescents with Disabilities.* Review any or all of the following reports: *The ICD Survey of Disabled Americans: Bringing Disabled Americans Into the Mainstream* (Louis Harris & Associates, 1986); *The ICD Survey II: Employing Disabled Americans* (Louis Harris & Associates, 1987); *The ICD Survey III: A Report Card on Special Education* (Louis Harris & Associates, 1989); *The N.O.D./Harris Survey on Employment of People with Disabilities* (Louis Harris & Associates, 1995); *What Happens Next? Trends in Postschool Outcomes of Youth with Disabilities* (Wagner, D'Amico, Marder, Newman, & Blackorby, 1992).

▶ Doing

Notice how many people with disabilities you see today. Take a piece of paper and note today's date. Write about the people you see. What do they look like? Are they using adaptive equipment (wheelchairs, canes or walkers, hearing aids, communication boards, etc.) or specialized services (interpreters, attendant services, sighted guides, etc.) to participate in society? Note what they are doing: working, playing, shopping, moving through space, and so on. How is each person like you?

CHAPTER 4

Career Counseling and Evaluation

Katherine was preparing for her internship with excitement, but also some fear and trepidation. She knew where she wanted to work—at the local nonprofit agency that provided services to women with mental health problems. She knew with whom she wanted to work—Marion Tesh, a woman about 10 years older than she and a licensed professional counselor. She knew what she wanted to do—provide those women with good career counseling and guidance so that they could become self-sufficient and feel better about themselves. She was comfortable with the counseling theory she would use as a basis for her intervention with her clients—a cognitive behavioral approach. What she was feeling most uncomfortable about was how she would assess her clients—what instruments would she use and would they be appropriate for all of her clientele?

Katherine made an appointment to meet with the vocational evaluator, Marcus Wilson, at the facility where she would be doing her internship in the spring semester. She thought it would be expedient and wise to find out now what assessment techniques were in use at the facility and determine how they would jive with her plans for counseling under Marion's supervision. She thought she would make an appointment with Marion following her observation and discussion with the vocational evaluator to be sure she understood how Marion used his findings. She left a message for Marion on her voice mail to that effect and prepared to meet Marcus. She reviewed the notes she had taken on vocational assessment last semester and made a list of the tests the lecturer had discussed. She then went to the library to read more about the tests in reference materials. She felt better knowing that she was at least vaguely familiar with a few of the better known instruments. She read about the *General Aptitude Test Battery* (GATB) (U.S. Department of Labor, 1970), the *Pennsylvania Bi-Manual Worksample* (Roberts, 1969), the *Strong Vocational Interest Blank* (Strong, Campbell, & Hansen, 1985), the *Kuder Occupational Interest Survey* (Kuder, 1960), and the *Non-Reading Aptitude Test Battery* (U.S. Department of Labor, 1971).

When she met with Marcus, Katherine was taken aback to discover that none of the vocational evaluation instruments she had read about were in use at the Women's Center. However, Marcus had reassured her that many of the tools the center used were similar to what she had read about. For example, the *Differential Aptitude Tests* (DAT) (Bennett, Seashore, & Wesman, 1982) has some subtests that parallel those of the GATB, the *Crawford Small Parts Dexterity Test* (Crawford & Crawford, 1975) is similar to the *Pennsylvania Bi-Manual Worksample* (Roberts, 1969), and so forth. The center's typical test battery for new clients consisted of the *Wechsler Adult Intelligence Scale–Revised* (Wechsler, 1981), the *Crawford Small Parts Dexterity Test* (Crawford & Crawford, 1975), the *Minnesota Clerical Test* (Andrew, Paterson, & Longstaff, 1961), the *Self-Directed Search* (SDS) (Holland, 1994), and the *Minnesota Multiphasic Personality Inventory* (Hathaway & McKinley, 1970). Although Marcus had access to the DAT, he said that he didn't use it with everyone because the reading level was too high for many of the center's clients. He indicated that the SDS was the most popular instrument according to the clients. When Katherine asked why, he suggested that she discuss that question with Marion because he wasn't sure.

Katherine had plenty of questions for Marion! How did she use the information she received from Marcus? Did she and the clients find the evaluation process helpful? Were there other tests that clients needed routinely? Were those written tests the sum total of the evaluation process? Would she have to interpret the tests for clients she and Marion would be counseling? Katherine set her appointment with Marion and made plans to do some further reading in the vocational evaluation area.

VOCATIONAL ASSESSMENT

The art of vocational assessment follows basically the same chronology as the art of career counseling. Many of the earlier vocational tests were designed to capture information about clients' interests and abilities so that counselors could provide guidance to clients in matching them with different kinds of jobs.

Traditional Vocational Assessment

Interest and Aptitude Tests

Traditional vocational assessment instruments fall into two major categories: interest tests and aptitude tests. These instruments are typically administered as paper-and-pencil tasks or at an interactive computer station. Some of the most widely used interest tests include the *Wide Range Interest–Opinion Test* (Jastak & Jastak, 1987), the *Strong Vocational Interest Blank* (Strong et al., 1985), the *Kuder Occupational Interest Survey* (Kuder, 1960), the *Career Assessment Inventory* (Johansson, 1986), and the *Self-Directed Search* (Holland, 1994). Some of the most popular aptitude tests include the *General Aptitude Test Battery* (U.S. Department of Labor, 1970), the *Non-Reading Aptitude Test Battery* (U.S. Department of Labor, 1971), the *Differential Aptitude Tests* (Bennett et al., 1982), the *Crawford Small Parts Dexterity Test* (Crawford & Crawford, 1975), the *Pennsylvania Bi-Manual Worksample* (Roberts, 1969), and the *Purdue Pegboard* (Tiffin, 1948). Readers interested in a detailed review of current vocational assessment instruments are encouraged to review Power's (1991) *A Guide to Vocational Assessment* and/or *The Mental Measurements Yearbook* (Rutgers University Staff, 1995).

Work Samples

In addition to the use of interest and aptitude tests, many vocational evaluators also use work samples that simulate jobs found in the labor market. Examples of work samples include the Singer Vocational Evaluation system (Singer Education Division/Career Systems, 80 Commerce Drive, Rochester, NY 14623), the Valpar system (Valpar Corp., 3801 East 34th Street, Tucson, AZ 85713), the JEVS work samples (Vocational Research Institute, 1624 Locust Street, Philadelphia, PA 19103), and the MICRO-TOWER System (MICRO-TOWER Services, ICD Rehabilitation and Research Center, 340 East 24th Street, New York, NY 10010). Work samples attempt to replicate industry-specific jobs. Clients being evaluated are asked to use the same tools and techniques an employed worker in such a job would use to perform routine duties. The client's performance is then judged based on comparisons with workers currently employed.

Nontraditional Vocational Assessment

Ecological Evaluations

Ecological evaluations are assessments performed in the environments where clients live, work, and attend school. They include information obtained from case folders, the perceptions of significant others, and observations over time of individuals engaged in their normal daily routines. It is important to note that initially and throughout the process the client is informed and actively participates in the evaluation process (to the maximum extent possible) and is provided with a summary report at the completion of the evaluation. In the following sections, the ecological evaluation process is described in detail.

The first stage of the ecological evaluation process is for the evaluator to review all existing client records. The evaluator reviews reports from classroom teachers, specialists (occupational and/or physical therapists, orientation and mobility specialists, speech and language therapists, technology specialists, psychologists, neurologists, etc.), medical doctors, the client's family members, and any client self-reports in the case folder. As the evaluator reviews the case record, it is important to note similarities and discrepancies evidenced in the case records. Questions that occur to the evaluator during the records review should be noted for future reference and verification. For example, if a client's case folder has a report indicating that the client has difficulty staying on task for longer than 15 minutes, the evaluator should note that fact and make plans to structure an observation to determine the current validity of that previous observation.

It is also important, for future reference, to note the dates of reports reviewed and names of those who generated the reports. If there is further identifying information about the authors of reports of interest, such as telephone numbers or addresses, that information can prove helpful. Having to return to a case folder to search for those kinds of details can be quite tedious and time-consuming. Needless to say, all information gleaned from an individual's case folder should be handled in the same confidential manner as the case folder itself.

Evaluators implementing the ecological assessment model spend considerable time observing their clients in a variety of settings. An observation checklist such as the one in Figure 4.1 should be used for consistency (see Appendix F for blackline master). Regardless of the format, some demographic and logistical information is critical to include: the name of the observer, the name of the client being observed, the date and time period of the observation, the site of the observation, and the names and roles of others present during the observation. It is essential to clearly define the tasks being performed and the skills the client uses to perform those tasks. Task descriptions should be understandable to other interested parties, including the client and client's family or other helpers. It is also important to note the kinds of work behaviors the evaluator sees in evidence at the observation sites.

The sites or places where an evaluator observes vary with the client's age and life complexity. For instance, a client who is in high school and preparing for transition into a work environment poses far different needs for observation than an adult who is reestablishing himself or herself into the labor market following a disabling accident. With the former, an evaluator should schedule observations (at different times and on different days of the week) in at least the following locations: in classes, in the cafeteria, during free time, at home or in the dorm, in therapy sessions, at work or work training site(s), on field trips, and in the community. With the latter, an evaluator should schedule observations

Observation Checklist

Client: _____

Observation date: _____ Observation time: _____

Placement: _____

Observer: _____

Task(s) performed/skill utilization: _____

_____

_____

_____

_____

_____

Work Behaviors Observed	Yes	No	N/A
Is punctual	☐	☐	☐
Initiates work	☐	☐	☐
Follows instructions	☐	☐	☐
Attends to task	☐	☐	☐
Attends to detail	☐	☐	☐
Cooperates	☐	☐	☐
Works consistently	☐	☐	☐
Dresses appropriately	☐	☐	☐
Solicits help, as needed	☐	☐	☐
Problem-solves tasks	☐	☐	☐
Interacts with coworkers	☐	☐	☐
Follows work rules	☐	☐	☐
Attends to safety concerns	☐	☐	☐
Completes tasks	☐	☐	☐
Puts tools/materials away	☐	☐	☐

Comments: List overall strengths and weaknesses. Make recommendations. Note level of supervision required to perform tasks assigned. For example, can client perform tasks independently when given verbal, signed, or written instructions? Can client perform with demonstration or tactual cues? How often does the client require prompting to stay on task? Does the client respond to certain people in the work environment more favorably than others? Note accommodations necessary for the client to perform optimally.

Figure 4.1. Observation Checklist.

in at least the following locations: at home, at work, in the community for recreation and leisure pursuits or volunteer work, in any training or rehabilitation settings, and the like.

In addition to client observations, an evaluator meets with personnel providing services to the client and notes where, when, and with whom he or she met; how to recontact each individual; and any other relevant details. Likewise, the evaluator contacts the client's family or significant others (with permission). At each meeting, the evaluator poses questions such as the following:

- What do you see as [name]'s strengths?
- What do you see as [name]'s weaknesses?
- What do you see [name] doing for a career?
- Where do you see [name] living?
- What kinds of supports (fiscal, transportation, housing, personal care, job coaching, access to information, or the like) do you think [name] will need to be successful in a work environment?

Finally, as a part of the ecological evaluation, the evaluator needs to do an extensive interview with the client. This may transpire in one or more sessions and should include some, but not necessarily all, of the following probes:

- Tell me a little bit about yourself.
- Tell me a little bit about your family.
- Where are you from? Do you plan to return to _____?
- What do you plan to do after completing high school (or other)?
- Where will you live and with whom?
- What kind of work do you want to do?
- How will you get a job?
- What skills have you developed during your academic career?
- What skills have you developed through your work experiences?
- What skills do you think you still need to develop?
- What are your greatest strengths?
- What are your greatest weaknesses?
- What do you like to do for fun?
- Have you worked? If yes, doing what? For whom?
- Do you have responsibilities at home? What are they?
- Have you done volunteer work? If yes, for whom? Doing what?
- What are your goals for this year? Five years from now? Ten years from now?
- What help will you need to achieve your goals?
- What 5 to 10 adjectives describe you best?
- What classes did you prefer in school?
- Do you prefer to work alone or with others?

- Do you prefer indoor or outdoor work environments?

- Do you like to work with people, data (information), or things?

- Do you want to work in a small, medium, or large company?

- Do you have specific concerns about work?

- What accommodations or adaptations will you need to perform at work?

In addition to asking some or all of the questions above, the evaluator attends to the following client attributes:

- Posture, gait, body language, and mannerisms

- Grooming, hygiene, and dress (stylishness, age-appropriateness, cleanliness, appropriateness to setting)

- Interactions with peers and with supervisors (including those at work sites; teachers, administrators, and dorm staff; parents and older family members)

- Generic social skills (social amenities such as saying "please," "thank you," and "you're welcome"; politely excusing oneself as appropriate; holding the door for others or helping carry things)

- Mobility to and from work as well as on the job site

- Manipulation of materials and tools, including maintenance

- Organizational skills

- Use of compensatory skills

- Use of aids and appliances

- Note-taking abilities (includes ability to retrieve information received)

- Self-initiating behaviors

- Level of supervision required to perform assigned tasks

As can be seen from these extensive listings, the ecological evaluation process is not a quick and easy way to find out about clients. Rather it is a comprehensive approach to analyzing skills and behaviors demonstrated by clients in natural environments. An ecological evaluation provides counselors and teachers with a wealth of information specific to a particular client. There is not a level of uniformity as in the traditional assessment format. For individuals with disabilities, the ecological approach enables the career counselor to focus on strengths and help clients determine whether their weaknesses can be accommodated with adaptive equipment or alternative methods, circumvented through job restructuring, or remediated through training or skill acquisition. Because few traditional vocational assessment tools have been normed on people with disabilities and there is great diversity in the disabled population, an ecological approach seems more viable. A process checklist is included as Figure 4.2 for the reader (see Appendix F for blackline master).

Situational Assessment

Situational assessment, like ecological evaluation, is performed on-site rather than in clinical testing environments. Some people use the terms situational assessment and ecological evaluation synonymously. However, there is a slight difference. Situational

Ecological Evaluation Process Checklist

Meet with the client to determine his or her vocational, social, academic, and independent living goals. It is important to spend time ascertaining the client's perception of his or her current performance and future needs in vocational, social, academic, and daily living skills areas. Inform the client of the nature of ecological evaluation and answer any questions. It is important that the client understand that, although you may observe him or her in activities without announcement, you will share with the client what you observed and the impressions you derived with him or her and/or his or her legal guardian/caregiver(s). (*Note:* This checklist can be combined with observation sheets by an evaluator.)

Review existing records (note date of reports and report writer)

Classroom teacher: _____

_____

_____

Specialists (orientation and mobility, occupational and physical therapy, speech–language therapy): _____

_____

_____

Psychological or neuropsychological: _____

_____

_____

Aptitude/achievement test results: _____

_____

_____

Medical reports: _____

_____

_____

Familial information: _____

_____

_____

Client's self-report: _____

_____

_____

(continues)

Figure 4.2. Ecological Evaluation Process Checklist.

©1997 by PRO-ED, Inc.

Observe (note location, others present, dates, and times)

Classes: _____

_____

_____

Cafeteria/restaurant: _____

_____

_____

Free time: _____

_____

_____

Dorm or home: _____

_____

_____

Therapy: _____

_____

_____

Work site: _____

_____

_____

Field trips/community activities: _____

_____

_____

Note dates, times, and locations of meetings with client and attach relevant outcomes (IWRP, IEP, ITP, IPP, other):

Meet with personnel providing services to client and note with whom you have met, how to recontact, date of contact, and any other relevant details:

Contact family members of student or significant others (attach copy of release of information) and note name, contact number and/or location, and date of contact:

Figure 4.2. Continued.

assessments are typically performed in a particular location (e.g., a work situation, a classroom situation). The evaluator may observe in the same location over a period of time or one time only. Ecological evaluations include observations performed in all areas of a client's life—work, home, school, community, and so forth—and are intended to extend over a period of time.

An example of a situational assessment protocol is the *Work Personality Profile* (WPP) (Bolton & Roessler, 1986). The WPP is described by the authors as a comprehensive observational tool that service providers can use to complete situational assessment of clients. The instrument consists of 58 items designed to capture a client's work performance. Work behaviors are noted as assets or problems. Scoring scales include acceptance of the work role, ability to profit from instruction or correction, work persistence, work tolerance, amount of supervision required, extent to which trainee seeks assistance from supervisor, degree of comfort or anxiety with supervisor, appropriateness of personal relations with supervisor, teamwork, ability to socialize with coworkers, social communication skills, task orientation, social skills, work motivation, work conformance, and personal presentation.

Assessment, like counseling, teaching, career guidance, and job placement, when used with adults does not lend itself to easy answers. There is not a right test or a right approach for everyone. There are many different ways to accomplish the same outcome goals: employment, quality of life, and high levels of self-esteem. Counselors need to work closely with their clients to determine what they perceive their needs to be and what their goals are, then to set objectives together to make their plans become a reality.

For individuals with severe developmental disabilities who are often advocacy-level clients, career counselors and vocational evaluators are encouraged to use nonstandardized testing procedures such as the ecological evaluation process and situational assessments.

Learning Activities

▶ **Reading**

Read about vocational assessment materials in either Power's (1991) book, *A Guide to Vocational Assessment,* or a comparable volume devoted to discussion of career education or vocational assessment tools. Also, consider reading Chapter 7 on ecological assessment strategies in *Supported Employment* by Powell et al. (1991). Powell and his colleagues have written specifically for counselors and instructors working with advocacy-level clients.

▶ **Doing**

Using the two forms included in this chapter, do an observation of a student or client with whom you are working or someone whom you know through your academic program.

SECTION 2

Career Counseling Content Areas

CHAPTER 5

Self-Awareness

Jason came to the rehabilitation agency to find out about a job seeking skills group that his friend, Eric, had mentioned to him. Eric told him the group might help him get organized with his job search. He understood that he, like others in the group, had to be on a rehabilitation counselor's caseload. He had registered with the Services for the Blind at his father's insistence before he graduated from high school, but he hadn't gone to see his counselor in months. Sometimes it felt weird going to the Services for the Blind office, because he could see pretty well. Although he couldn't drive, he could easily walk or ride his bicycle almost anywhere. If he needed to go someplace that was out of his neighborhood, he took a bus or cab or bummed a ride with family or friends.

On the day of his appointment, he took a bus because the rehabilitation agency was well out of his neighborhood. He'd lived in the city all his life and didn't consider getting around to be a hassle. He was scheduled to meet his counselor, Ed Hanson, at the agency at 3:00 P.M. He arrived a few minutes early and read while he waited to see Ed (it sure was nice that he didn't have to call him Mr. Hanson like a school teacher!).

Ed thanked him for being on time. Jason told him he wanted to join the job seeking skills group that his friend Eric had attended. He said he wasn't having much luck finding a job on his own and that maybe he needed some help. They chatted about the group. Ed explained that it was a contracted service, meaning that a private counselor facilitated the group for the agency. The group met at a community activity center near downtown, and a new class was forming to start within the next few weeks. He said he would make the referral, if Jason was committed to attending.

Ed asked Jason if he was satisfied with his life. Jason thought. He wondered, "*Am* I satisfied with my life?" Jason thought about the things going on in his life: his parents, upset with him for goofing off rather than going to school or work; his grandparents acting as if nothing was wrong; his friends now distant—in school in other states or married with children, except Eric who would ask if he'd followed up on his suggestion. He said, "No, I am *not* satisfied with my life. I think I can do better. I want to go to work. Can this group help me? Do you think I ought to try it?"

Ed suggested that Jason meet with the group facilitator, Dr. Winston, before making a final decision about the group. Ed said that he thought the group might be a good idea rather than Jason's simply meeting with Ed periodically. He asked Jason if he had particular jobs in mind in which he was interested. Jason really didn't—any job would do! Ed said "any" job was too broad, that he had to have in mind specific jobs, if he was to keep an eye open for possibilities. He said Jason needed to figure out what he had to offer and where his talents would match up best. Jason thought he should ask Dr. Winston about that.

PROMOTING SELF-AWARENESS

Counselors should start with self-awareness activities as quickly as possible to facilitate the career planning process for their clients. Ideally, both self-awareness activities and vocational exploration activities (which are covered in the next chapter) should be introduced as soon as possible so that clients can work in both areas simultaneously. Handouts are provided in Appendix A to facilitate clients' efforts to gain self-awareness.

In career and life planning, self-awareness is indicated by a thorough knowledge of interests, abilities, values, and liabilities. Interests include what an individual enjoys or likes to do—at home, in school, for fun, voluntarily in the community, and so forth. Abilities are demonstrable skills, talents, or special things (i.e., aptitudes) that an individual possesses and can do well. Values are based on what an individual believes to be right or wrong. Values differ from person to person and culture to culture. People's values or beliefs have intrinsic worth to them. Liabilities are the things an individual cannot do well or perceives as barriers.

In addition to knowing how one feels about oneself, an individual who demonstrates high levels of self-awareness understands how others see him or her and uses feedback from others' observations to analyze the impact of his or her behavior on others. In other words, such individuals relate well to other people and can use their feedback constructively. They pay attention to feedback from others and incorporate it into their overall understanding of themselves.

People who are self-aware typically are able and willing to set goals. They set both personality and achievement goals. Personality goals are those goals individuals set because they want to change something about themselves for self-improvement. For example, personality goals include becoming more assertive, more outgoing, or more patient. Achievement goals are those goals people set because they want to acquire an object, gain a credential, receive an award, or the like. Examples of achievement goals include acquiring a new car, successfully completing a course, and earning a diploma. Details about both achievement and personality goals are contained in the sections below. Both kinds of goals are critical to life success (Carkhuff, 1993; Carkhuff & Berenson, 1977; Means & Roessler, 1976).

Description of Goals

Achievement Goals

Achievement goals are finite—they have identifiable starting and ending points in time. The attainment of an achievement goal usually results in the acquisition of a tangible item: a diploma, an object one desires such as a house or car, an award, or something similar. Once an individual has identified what he or she wants to achieve or acquire, the time frame for achieving the outcome can be defined in terms of how much time, money, or energy needs to be expended to acquire that "thing one wants." Some achievement goals can be accomplished in fairly short order; others take longer. For example, completing a class successfully may take only a semester; however, acquiring a degree may take 4 or 5 years of study. Either way, the individual pursuing the goal knows from the beginning what is required (in terms of resources such as time, money, or energy) to accomplish the goal.

Short-term achievement goals make up the to-do lists of everyday life. As many time management experts advise, making a list of the things one needs to accomplish on a daily basis is a crucial component of successful time management. In addition to writing out what one needs to accomplish, it is important to prioritize the things on the to-do list. One should determine what is the most important thing, second, third, and so forth—not what is easiest or quickest to accomplish, but what is truly the first priority. A to-do list is essential to career and life planning. People who want to make the most of their time and energy use this technique (Covey, 1989; Means & Roessler, 1976).

On a daily basis, individuals need to define what "little" tasks they could do to make their lives move more smoothly. These tasks are the kinds of chores that, if left undone, continue to pile up and cause great duress ultimately (e.g., piles of laundry or dishes, papers that need to be written and turned in). In addition to daily details, steps toward larger goals also need to be included on to-do lists (e.g., visits to the library for research purposes, picking up job applications in an area of interest).

Some achievement goals take substantially longer than other goals. For example, it takes a considerable amount of time, effort, and money to pursue a degree program at the baccalaureate or master's level. Long-term achievement goals include academic pursuits; job advancement efforts; major projects such as writing a book or renovating a property; and saving for an expensive item such as a piece of jewelry, equipment, tools, a vehicle, home, or the like. It may take months or years to acquire the thing or reach the goal one has in mind. The key to success with achievement goals is to clearly define the desired outcome and the intermediate steps to completion, then to steadily work through each step until the desired outcome is achieved.

Personality Goals

Personality goals involve change within oneself. These goals demand internal refocusing and are often extremely difficult to achieve and time-consuming. With a personality goal, one determines that changing something within one's person or personality would make the individual a better person. Personality goals are typically long-term goals. Individuals undertake personality goals because they are unhappy with their current situation or desire self-improvement. Often, people feel that their current behavior patterns are not producing the desired results.

Clients may report that they are unhappy, lonely, misunderstood, taken advantage of, upset, angry, or suffering from some other ill. Pain or discomfort is what motivates most people to adopt personality goals. Clients typically want to change something about themselves to feel more comfortable or satisfied with their lives. Personality goals do not result in tangible "things"; rather the results produced are internal change factors. People who achieve their personality goals feel better about themselves.

Personality goals may elicit negative reactions from the people closest to the person trying to change. This is because others, particularly those who know the client best, have grown accustomed to the behavior currently being demonstrated and they don't know what to make of new, different behavior. Often, the change being evidenced is not what is expected or desired from the individual. To minimize the consequences of others' negative reactions, it is important to share with significant others the desired personality change being undertaken.

Figure 5.1 provides a succinct overview of these three categories of goals: daily goals, achievement goals, and personality goals. The figure shows graphically the differences in time to complete, the frequency of evaluation needed, and the ease of accomplishment for the types of goals. The challenge for each person is to set realistic goals in each of the different categories.

COUNSELING STRATEGIES

The following sections detail counseling strategies that are particularly suitable to group settings. Working with clients in group settings is encouraged when possible because of the valuable information swapping that frequently occurs (Corey & Corey, 1992). However, many of the suggested activities can also be used for individual work.

Goal Differentiation			
	Types of Goals		
Means of Measurement	Daily Goals	Achievement Goals	Personality Goals
Time To Complete	Short-term completion	Time-limited to completion	Long-term commitment
Evaluation Frequency	Daily evaluation	Periodic evaluation (finite)	Periodic evaluation (ongoing)
Ease of Accomplishment	Easiest to do	More difficult to undertake, but time required to finish or acquire is predictable	Requires extensive effort over long periods of time and time required may not be predictable

Figure 5.1. Goal differentiation.

Values Clarification Exercises

Values clarification exercises are designed to help clients explore and define what they consider to be important. Exercises such as those detailed by Raths, Harmin, and Simon (1966), Means and Roessler (1976), DeVito (1995), or Simon, Howe, and Kirschenbaum (1995) can easily be incorporated into group meetings of job seekers.

An example from the values clarification approach (Simon et al., 1995), the lifeline activity, has participants document five accomplishments from birth to present and five aspirations from present to anticipated date of death. This activity encourages values clarification by having participants write down the things of most importance to them in their lives. Likewise, an epitaph-writing exercise in the same curriculum works well in terms of participants analyzing personal values. In the epitaph-writing activity, participants write out what they would like said of them after death in terms of how they lived their lives. These activities can be shared in a group process or used in individual counseling sessions.

Some values clarification exercises elicit strong feelings from group members. For example, an activity described by Raths and his colleagues (1966) has participants look at a group of make-believe characters who have survived an atomic blast. Group members must choose from the make-believe group (which has members of different races, religions, sexual orientation, and other attributes that lend themselves to a discussion of values) a smaller number who will be allowed to survive in the aftermath of the supposed atomic blast. Invariably, some group members feel strongly about saving certain members of the make-believe group over others, and this can lead to rather heated discussions. In such situations, it is important that the group facilitator use his or her counseling skills to manage the group process in a way that allows each participant to feel comfortable and significant.

Interest Checklists and Tests

Many of the commercially available interest tests, such as the *Strong Vocational Interest Blank* (Strong, Campbell, & Hansen, 1985), the *Self-Directed Search* (SDS) (Holland, 1994), and the *Kuder Occupational Interest Survey* (Kuder, 1960), can be administered to individuals with disabilities with a minimum of modification (Power, 1991). For individuals with visual disabilities, the SDS is available in braille. Nonreaders with adequate residual vision to discriminate pictorial information may benefit from doing the *Revised Reading-Free Vocational Interest Inventory* (Becker, 1981). Handout A.1 in Appendix A is a tool the counselor can use to stimulate clients' thoughts about their interests.

Aside from standardized tests, Friel and Carkhuff (1974), in their book *The Art of Developing a Career*, encourage counselors to follow their six-step interviewing model to assist clients in determining and expanding their interest areas. Briefly, these six steps are as follows:

1. Ask clients open-ended questions (e.g., What do you enjoy doing in your spare time?) to help identify their interests.

2. Help clients explore their values by asking questions (e.g., What kinds of things were important to you when you were in school or working?).

3. Help clients organize their values into intellectual, physical, and emotional/interpersonal areas.

4. Help clients categorize interest information into people-oriented or thing-oriented occupations.

5. Help clients determine which interest category best matches their values.

6. Identify training and job requirements essential to employment areas congruent with clients' values and interests.

Aptitude Testing

A few aptitude tests, such as the *Pennsylvania Bi-Manual Worksample* (Roberts, 1969), the *Comprehensive Vocational Evaluation System* (Dial et al., 1992), and the *McCarron–Dial Evaluation Systems* (McCarron & Dial, 1986), are appropriate for and normed with people who are disabled. In addition, some tests such as the *Crawford Small Parts Dexterity Test* (Crawford & Crawford, 1975) and the *Purdue Pegboard* (Tiffin, 1948), can be adapted for persons with most disabilities. Some rehabilitation facilities provide work samples, which simulate jobs in the community, to evaluate client aptitude. However, such samples can be difficult to maintain in relation to an ever-changing labor market. Other strategies for determining aptitudes include informal job tryout periods, client's self-evaluation, observation on previous job sites and in classroom settings, and review of transcripts and work history (Power, 1991). Many contemporary career counselors (e.g., Bolles, 1997) encourage job seekers to develop listings of their personal attributes, which can provide insight into clients' aptitudes. Handout A.2 can be used by clients to generate listings of their skills.

Special Issues

Honest, open feedback to people with disabilities is essential. Information concerning appearance (person and clothing) and behavior (including the effect of behaviors on others) is critical for gaining further insight into what is working for and against individuals. Feedback can be solicited from significant others, such as family members, counselors, teachers, and/or peers. However, some clients may require instruction on how to ask for feedback from others. Rather than reliance on facial expressions and body language, clients with visual impairments and those with processing difficulties require verbal explanations of feelings evoked by interactions with them. Likewise, clear verbal descriptions of visual data, including videotapes, films, television, and newspapers, can provide clients who have difficulty interpreting visual information with a more accurate understanding of the world in which they live and work.

Like others, people with disabilities need and want to know what others like about them. For counselors, this means taking time to point out what attributes clients are demonstrating that will serve them well in the labor market. If there are areas that need improvement, counselors should point them out in a way that is not hurtful and leaves plenty of room for facilitated growth. This means focusing on behaviors that are amenable to change and not personal attributes that are inherent. Handout A.3 is a summary sheet for clients to complete once they have completed the activities in this chapter.

· ·

What Jason did . . .

Dr. Winston told Jason about the job seeking skills group. It was designed to run for 4 weeks. The group would meet at the community college for 6 hours a day, from 8:30 A.M. to 3:30 P.M., Monday through Friday. The first 2 weeks were designed to be broken into half days: half a day spent in a content-specific lecture and discussion period, followed by individual application exercises, and half a day spent in group counseling focusing on communication skills, problem-solving skills, values clarification, and goal setting activities. In the third week, the group would work together on job seeking techniques: reviewing openings, filling out applications and sharing them with group members for feedback, practicing interviewing skills, doing videotaped interviews, critiquing interviews, and role-playing difficult situations that might come up on the job or in the process of searching for work.

If clients had job interviews, they would be excused from classroom activities. No other absences were acceptable. The first 3 weeks of the program were fairly set. During the fourth week, the clients would apply what they had learned by scheduling appointments and interviews, seeking leads, filling out applications, and applying for appropriate jobs. The faculty made themselves available during the fourth week to practice interviewing techniques or to review paperwork. That was also the time when a final case staffing would be scheduled with the referring counselor to discuss progress and negotiate any further assistance needed.

Jason said he was prepared to undertake the process. Dr. Winston said the group would begin the following Monday and that the first content area to be covered was self-awareness. He said that becoming aware of one's own strengths and weaknesses was the place to start in order to make a good decision about what career or job a person matched up with best. It made sense to Jason, and he went home feeling that he had made a good decision when he decided to join the group.

Learning Activities

▶ **Reading**

Read or browse one or more of the following books: *Where Do I Go From Here With My Life?* by Crystal and Bolles (1974), *The Three Boxes of Life and How To Get Out of Them* by Bolles (1978), *Please Understand Me* by Keirsey and Bates (1984), *Do What You Are* by Tieger and Barron-Tieger (1992), and *Do What You Love, the Money Will Follow* by Sinetar (1987).

▶ **Doing**

The following activities are designed to provide you with valuable information about yourself. These same activities are excellent tools for helping clients explore themselves.

1. On a piece of paper, write your name and today's date. Then write at least 10 *interests* that you have (at home, at school, at play), not necessarily in order of preference. Write 10 *abilities* (i.e., your best skills and talents at home, at school, and at play). Next, write 10 *values* (i.e., the things in which you believe most strongly). For many people, this is the most difficult part because people are rarely asked to label their values. In fact, you or some of your clients may need the assistance of a values word list, such as the one shown in Figure 5.2 (see Appendix F for blackline master). It is important to rank order your values once you have captured them on paper; however, you may prefer to simply list the activities now without doing the rank ordering, and then to think about what you've written and return to the list later to do the rank ordering.

The final part of this activity is to write out three liabilities. It is critical that you be honest with yourself about your liabilities or perceived barriers to employment. If you cannot think of any difficulties or problems you may encounter as you look

---

Values Word List

Freedom	Recognition	Kindness
Creativity	Self-direction	Flexibility
Family life	Interdependence	Routines
Honesty	Caretaking	Education
Happiness	Cheerfulness	Serenity
Learning	Morality	Orderliness
Openness	Craftsmanship	Mobility
Aesthetics	Adventure	Friendship
Joy	Wisdom	Independence
Helpfulness	Wealth	Regard
Frugality	Solitude	Fame
Leadership	Religion	Affection
Athletics	Health	Privacy
Strength	Integrity	Fortune
Responsibility	Security	Nature
Beauty	Respect	Spirituality
Cleanliness	Generosity	Relationships

Figure 5.2. Values Word List.

for work or career change, ask friends and family what they perceive to be your liabilities or weaknesses. Capture their thoughts on paper and consider whether their perceptions are accurate. If you decide that their concerns are valid, list them as liabilities.

2. Put your lifeline on paper. Draw a line across the top of a piece of paper. On the far left end of the line, write your birthdate. Somewhere along the line (depending on how old you are when you complete this activity), write today's date. On the far right end of the line, write the date of your anticipated demise. Below the lifeline, note five accomplishments you have experienced to date (e.g., learning to read or ride a bike or swim or sing; earning an award or winning a trophy or certificate; establishing a relationship or having responsibility for a family; building a home or acquiring a car). Next, note five things you would like to accomplish before you die.

CHAPTER 6

Vocational Selection

Jason was excited about starting the job readiness group and arrived on time the day the group was scheduled to begin. There were seven other participants in the group: a man who had been badly burned in an accident and was about 45 years old, a man who said he had mental health problems and seemed about 30 years old, a guy his age who had hurt his back in a car accident, another guy about his age or maybe a little older who was totally blind, a woman who was visually impaired and about 30 years old, a girl about his age who said she had learning disabilities, and a woman who was maybe 45 or 50 who said she had multiple sclerosis. He had never been with such an assortment of people. They seemed to have only two things in common: They were all unemployed and they were all rehabilitation clients.

Dr. Winston, Jim as he preferred to be called, was a neat man, who seemed genuinely interested in all of them. He had carefully explained the group's purpose and discussed the schedule for the next 4 weeks. He had participated in their introductions this morning and talked about himself openly. He was married and had two kids in elementary school. He wasn't a medical doctor. His degree was in rehabilitation counseling. Jason didn't even realize there was such a thing as a doctorate in rehabilitation counseling!

Jim had given them homework, too. Jason was to write down his interests, abilities, values, and liabilities. This information was going to get them started on what Jim called their self-analysis process. They would do different activities in class to help them investigate themselves during this first week. They would also begin investigating the labor market. Jim called that process vocational selection and said the overriding objective in preparing to go to work was to make a good match between oneself and a job.

UNDERSTANDING VOCATIONAL SELECTION

Vocational selection involves individuals in the process of determining what careers and jobs are of interest to them. During the vocational selection stage, career counseling clients learn how to use career exploration materials. They learn how to research local and national labor market demands and trends. Individuals study how to do job analyses (Handout B.1 in Appendix B) and how to perform a discrepancy analysis (Handout B.2). Using the discrepancy analysis procedure, clients compare themselves to job and career choices on paper. Outcome goals that clients can anticipate achieving by working through this stage include

- establishing short-term and long-term career objectives,
- understanding how abilities and qualifications match available jobs, and
- knowing how selected jobs relate to career objectives.

In summary, the process of vocational selection results in an awareness of available jobs and career paths. Vocational awareness is indicated by knowledge of employers available in one's home community who hire for positions that match, as closely as possible, one's abilities, interests, and values. Identified jobs have been analyzed to determine that fiscal and physical needs can be met. Finally, alternative jobs are identified that are related to life/career goals and can be sought in the event that one's primary choice is unavailable.

Job Classification Resources

To assist clients with researching career and employment opportunities, counselors must have a well-developed sense of the structure of the labor market. What kinds of jobs are available and where are these jobs located? The three most widely used general resources for job classification and information are the U.S. Department of Labor's *Dictionary of Occupational Titles* (DOT; 1991), *Guide for Occupational Exploration* (GOE; 1979), and *Occupational Outlook Handbook* (OOH; 1996). Each of these resources is described in detail in the following sections.

Dictionary of Occupational Titles

The DOT is the most comprehensive listing of jobs being performed in the United States. Approximately 20,000 jobs are described in the DOT. To use the DOT effectively to assist clients who are researching career opportunities, counselors need a working knowledge of this reference text. The DOT is divided into occupational categories, divisions, and groups. The nine major occupational categories referenced in the DOT, with their numeric identifiers, are as follows:

0/1 Professional, Technical, and Managerial Occupations	5 Processing Occupations
2 Clerical and Sales Occupations	6 Machine Trades Occupations
3 Service Occupations	7 Bench Work Occupations
4 Farming , Fishery, Forestry, and Related Occupations	8 Structural Work Occupations
	9 Miscellaneous Occupations

Each job is designated by a unique, nine-digit code. The first three digits identify the job's occupational group. The first digit designates the broad occupational category, the first and second digits in combination equate to occupational divisions, and the first three digits together define the occupational group. The middle three digits make up the worker function ratings of tasks performed in that job. A separate digit, from 0 (*most complex*) to 8 (*least complex*), identifies a worker's involvement with each of the following: data (fourth digit), people (fifth digit), and things (sixth digit). The last three digits of the occupational code differentiate a specific job from all other jobs with the same first six digits.

For example, the job of airplane-flight attendant has a numeric DOT code of 352.367-010. The occupational code is translated as follows:

- *Occupational Group* (352): The 3 represents service occupations; the 5 indicates that this division includes jobs in which the workers provide personal services, such as stewards and hostesses; and the 2 means this group is designated as specific to helping travelers or working in hotels and restaurants.

- *Worker Functions* (367): The 3 relates to the worker's level of functioning with data (compiling: gathering information and carrying out prescribed actions); the 6 relates to people functions (speaking–signaling: exchanging information with others); and the 7 indicates functioning with things (handling: moving or carrying objects and selecting tools or objects).

- *Differentiating Number* (010): These three numbers simply separate this job from any other jobs classified as 352.367. There is no inherent meaning to the numeric code that follows the first six digits other than to differentiate the job within its category.

Although the DOT was revised in 1991, it has not been entirely reworked since 1977. However, several changes in the 1991 revision are noteworthy. Some job descriptions have been rewritten, 844 new occupations have been included, and 208 outdated job descriptions have been deleted. The following are the most significant changes in the revised edition:

- GOE codes are included for cross-referencing.

- Strength factor codes are listed with each job description, as are RML (Reasoning, Math, and Language) codes and SVP (Specific Vocational Preparation) codes.

- The date of the most recent update is given.

- A new occupational division (03) has been created for computer-related occupations under the 0/1 occupational category (professional, technical, and managerial).

Guide for Occupational Exploration

Like the DOT, the GOE categorizes occupations; however, it divides job descriptions into occupational interest areas:

01	Artistic	07	Business Detail
02	Scientific	08	Selling
03	Plants and Animals	09	Accommodating
04	Protective	10	Humanitarian
05	Mechanical	11	Leading-influencing
06	Industrial	12	Physical-performing

This strategy enables clients to investigate occupations within their interest areas, whereas with the DOT clients typically use a job title to initiate their research. Therefore, the GOE is especially helpful with clients whose knowledge of careers is limited.

In addition to its merit as an interest-driven research tool, the GOE is correlated to the DOT and the *General Aptitude Test Battery* (U.S. Department of Labor, 1970), the U.S. Employment Service's interest and aptitude tests. Its interest areas can also be related to the occupational categories in Holland's (1994) *Self-Directed Search*.

Occupational Outlook Handbook

The OOH categorizes jobs in much the same manner as the DOT; however, it covers fewer jobs (approximately 250) in far more detail than the DOT does. The OOH uses the DOT numeric codes for all the jobs it includes. The following categories of jobs are covered in the OOH:

- Executive, Administrative, and Managerial Occupations

- Professional Specialty Occupations

- Technicians and Related Support Occupations
- Marketing and Sales Occupations
- Administrative Support Occupations, Including Clerical
- Service Occupations
- Agriculture, Forestry, Fishing, and Related Occupations
- Mechanics, Installers, and Repairers
- Construction Trades and Extractive Occupations
- Production Occupations
- Transportation and Material Moving Occupations
- Handlers, Equipment Cleaners, Helpers, and Laborers
- Job Opportunities in the Armed Forces

The major differences in the OOH and the previously mentioned resources, the DOT and the GOE, are the number of jobs described and the amount of information covered. The OOH describes only 250 jobs rather than the thousands of jobs described in the other two resources; however, the OOH provides a great deal more detail about each job it covers and is updated every other year. Included in each job description are the following: information concerning the nature of the work; working conditions; employment locations; training, other qualifications, and advancement; job outlook; earnings; related occupations; and sources of additional information.

Counseling Strategies

The following sections present a variety of methods that can be used in individual or group counseling sessions. Although the processes can easily be introduced in group settings, specific job analyses and the discrepancy analysis process lend themselves to individual work. The level of independence demonstrated by clients in researching and analyzing job choices gives the counselor concrete evidence of work performance.

To efficiently capture critical information from job reference materials, it is important that clients understand what information to pull from the resources. By using a job analysis form, such as that shown in Figure 6.1 (see Appendix F for blackline master), a client can know he or she is capturing the same type of information for all jobs of interest.

Instruction in Research Methodology

Clients should first be introduced to general occupational research materials, such as the *Dictionary of Occupational Titles*, the *Guide for Occupational Exploration*, and the *Occupational Outlook Handbook* (all of these resources are available on computer disks, CD-ROM, or audiotapes, as well as printed formats). The counselor should introduce clients to the layout and coding system of each of these generic job resources. It may also be helpful to provide examples. The counselor should encourage clients to take notes and jot down questions that arise as they read these general reference materials, using the job analysis form. The counselor also should teach clients how to access these reference materials through local public library systems and explain where related reference materials may be located.

Job Analysis Form

Name: _____ Date: _____

Job Title: _____

Numeric Code (from *Dictionary of Occupational Titles* or *Guide for Occupational Exploration*): _____

Purpose (reason job exists): _____
_____
_____
_____

Setting (location and environment): _____
_____
_____
_____

Major Tasks (job duties): _____
_____
_____
_____
_____
_____
_____
_____

Qualifications (experience, education, special skills, licensure, etc.): _____
_____
_____
_____
_____
_____
_____
_____
_____
_____
_____

(continues)

Figure 6.1. Job Analysis Form.

List employers in your community who hire people to do the job in which you're interested:

Company: _____

Address: _____

_____

Contact Person: _____

Phone Number: _____

Company: _____

Address: _____

_____

Contact Person: _____

Phone Number: _____

Company: _____

Address: _____

_____

Contact Person: _____

Phone Number: _____

Company: _____

Address: _____

_____

Contact Person: _____

Phone Number: _____

Company: _____

Address: _____

_____

Contact Person: _____

Phone Number: _____

Company: _____

Address: _____

_____

Contact Person: _____

Phone Number: _____

Figure 6.1. Continued.

Reference materials with more specific information about certain jobs or career choices, such as the *Occupational Outlook Quarterly* and the *Monthly Labor Review*, published by the U.S. Department of Labor (Bureau of Labor Statistics, Washington, DC 20212), and *Career Opportunities News*, a newsletter published by Garrett Park Press (P.O. Box 190-B, Garrett Park, MD 20896), may also be helpful to clients as they research areas of interest. Local Chambers of Commerce, Better Business Bureaus, state employment commissions, rehabilitation agencies, business schools, community colleges, and universities often have both general and specific job reference materials in their libraries and, in the case of vocational schools and institutes of higher education, in their placement offices. Clients also need to know how to use specialized services such as regional Library of Congress depositories and Recording for the Blind and Dyslexic. Some consumer organizations, such as American Council of the Blind, Association for Retarded Citizens (now Arc), National Association of the Deaf, National Federation of the Blind, and United Cerebral Palsy, also maintain information files on jobs being performed by or available to individuals with disabilities. The *Directory of National Information Sources on Disabilities* (National Institute on Disability and Rehabilitation Research, 1994) provides a listing of information resources related to specific disabilities.

Once clients have exhausted the print (taped, brailled, and/or computerized) resources on jobs, they should focus on answering questions they have generated that are specific to them. For example, they can interview workers in jobs like those they are interested in to find out whether the book descriptions accurately reflect how those jobs are being performed in their communities. They may be curious if people with similar disabilities have been able to secure such jobs and, if so, what accommodations or adaptations have been necessary for them to perform successfully. Techniques for gathering specific information about jobs follow.

Informational Interviewing

Bolles introduced the concept of informational interviewing to the general public in his classic job seeking skills manual, *What Color Is Your Parachute?* (1997, updated annually). In this book, Bolles encourages job hunters to seek out and set interviews with individuals in the labor force whose jobs match their own career interests. With a list of prepared questions in hand, the job seeker collects information about work in a chosen area; however, he or she seeks only information and not employment through this process. Actual job interviews follow informational interviews in the job seeking sequence.

Job Shadowing

The job shadowing activity is exactly what it sounds like: An individual follows someone during the performance of his or her typical work duties and responsibilities. Often, prospective workers shadow an employee for a number of days. This strategy enables an individual to make a well-informed decision regarding a potential work role. Student teaching experiences, counseling practica, residencies, and internships are all advanced levels of job shadowing.

Volunteering

Clients still in a quandary, after having made an earnest attempt at job researching, may need to volunteer in a position they would like to consider. In addition to clarifying career choices, volunteer positions can provide references, supervised work experiences, or a documented track record for those clients with poor job histories or limited work experience.

Discrepancy Analysis

Clients who have completed job research activities are ready to perform the discrepancy analysis process. In this process, a client performs a self-evaluation and writes down the results (using a format similar to the self-assessment summary sheet, Handout A.3). Then, the client completes a series of job analyses (typically 3 to 5 analyses using a format similar to the job analysis form, Handout B.1). Finally, the client compares each job (what it offers, what it demands) to himself or herself (what he or she wants, what he or she can give). The differences between the two (job and self) are known as discrepancies. Once discrepancies have been identified, the client must determine if he or she can and is willing to resolve them. For example, a job may demand a graduate degree and the client may welcome an opportunity for more schooling; in such an instance, the discrepancy is amenable to change. In another instance, the client may be unwilling to return to school; in this case, the discrepancy is not amenable to change and, therefore, would rule out the prospective job seeker.

Using the discrepancy analysis procedure encourages clients to make objective decisions about their life and career goals. Counselors do not superimpose their values on clients by falling into the trap of telling clients what they can or should do with their lives.

Special Issues

Voluminous reference materials and limited support staff to facilitate access to generic vocational selection materials make using them difficult and time-consuming for clients. For nonprint readers, accessing routinely printed information, particularly newspapers (business sections, special supplements, classified advertising) and postings of help wanted signs, can be a major source of frustration. Such visual input informs the curious of how popular certain positions are, how frequently positions turn over, how well certain companies are doing fiscally, where budgeted monies will be appropriated, and such. Some clients will be able to use computerized reading machines to access some of these materials. However, many clients who are visually impaired will have to either rely on the reports of others or solicit such information by phone or in person.

Likewise, observing environments from afar to ascertain whether one wishes to work in such a place is severely restricted without distance vision. Once again, clients must either solicit information from others and rely on their perceptions or visit and ask questions in person. Information interviewing techniques—that is, approaching a prospective employer with a detailed list of questions about the work environment and duties—can help in securing input about companies being considered. However, turning around and asking for a job from an employer one has just grilled is, needless to say, not a recommended tactic. Therefore, to scrutinize a prospective working environment, a person without vision may do better to ask as many people as possible for their opinions. Ideally, clients should ask some current employees of the firm of interest for their insights.

Inadequate social networks may contribute to deficient vocational selection behaviors (Temelini & Fesko, 1997). If a client has been living in isolation from the community at large or in a very restricted environment, knowledge of the local job market and people involved in it will likely be limited. Likewise, due in part to the low incidence of disability in the working-age population, people with impairments may encounter significant numbers of individuals who will have stereotypic views of what they can and cannot do.

• •

What Jason did . . .

That evening after his first job readiness meeting, Jason wrote down his interests, abilities, values, and liabilities. The interests he listed were sports—basketball, baseball, and football; music; bicycling; girls; skating; going to the mall; computer games; and using computers to get information (via Internet). The abilities he listed were good listener; get along with other people; read; organize; repair bikes; help with yardwork; manage money; take care of self and room; computer skills—word processing, games, and e-mail. His values, which he rank ordered, were (1) independence, (2) security, (3) family, (4) friends, (5) religion, (6) freedom, (7) loyalty, (8) honesty, (9) health, and (10) privacy. He wrote the following liabilities: inexperienced, limited vision, sensitive to sun, and no college. He knew his parents were hoping he would go to college, but he couldn't get enthusiastic about it. He told them that he needed to take a few years off and work before considering college further. They were disappointed and not very happy with his having just "hung around" for the last few months; however, they were delighted that he'd signed up to participate in the job readiness group. It helped that the group met at the community college.

As Jason did the homework assignment, he thought about the other things the group had done at the meeting. The morning had been taken up with the introductions and Jim's explanation of what to expect. He'd handed out class rules and the requirements for receiving a certificate of completion. Jim expected joblike behaviors: Participants were expected to be present everyday, show up on time, take breaks and lunch only as designated, follow instructions, cooperate with the instructor, and turn in assignments on time. (Getting back on a schedule would be good for him!) Following his orientation to the class rules and regulations, Jim showed the group members some of the reference materials about jobs: the DOT, the OOH, and the GOE. In the afternoon, the group had talked at length about problem solving and goal setting—it really felt like a "counseling" group. From the way Jim had described things, each afternoon session would be like today's, with members discussing goals, solving problems, talking about values, and learning good communication skills. The morning sessions were reserved for exploring career options and learning how to get and keep a job. The schedule indicated that tomorrow's topic would be "The Perfect Job." Jason wondered, "Is there such a beast?"

Learning Activities

▶ Reading

Thoroughly familiarize yourself with the *Dictionary of Occupational Titles* (DOT), *Guide for Occupational Exploration* (GOE), and *Occupational Outlook Handbook* (OOH). In the DOT, be sure to read the introduction, which describes in detail the parts of the occupational definition and how to find an occupational title and code. Also read through the DOT appendixes, which provide you with information about revisions to the DOT, explanations of worker functions, information found in the definition trailer (date of last update, specific vocational preparation, general educational development, physical demands and strength rating, and the GOE code), and how to use the DOT in job placement. Likewise, in the GOE, be sure to read the introductory information and the appendixes. The OOH is designed differently from the DOT and the GOE. There are not true appendixes; however, at the end of the book there is information about job opportunities in the armed forces, summary data for jobs not listed in the main section, a cross-reference to the DOT, and an alphabetical index to jobs covered in the OOH. Introductory material can be found at the beginning of the OOH, as in the DOT and GOE.

▶ Doing

Make copies of the job analysis form (Handout B.1 in Appendix B). Choose two or three jobs of interest to you and research them, using the reference materials described in this chapter. Take notes as you complete your research on the job analysis forms (one for each job you have chosen). Select two or three jobs that you think will be of interest to clients with whom you will be working and research them as well. By researching some of the jobs you think might be of interest to potential clients, you can begin to build a stash of samples. It may be necessary to show clients how to gather information and/or how to sort through information they have gathered. Using the job analysis form, clients can start the vocational selection process.

CHAPTER 7

Job Seeking Skills

Jason felt excited about the jobs he had chosen to pursue. The first week in the job readiness program had been intense, but he'd narrowed down his interest areas. He had researched three jobs: sound technician, sporting goods salesman, and software developer. He realized that the sales job was probably the only one of the three for which he was qualified without further schooling. He would do some informational interviews about sound technician and software developer jobs, but planned to focus his job seeking on retail sales. He planned to try sporting goods shops first and music stores second.

With Jim's help he was ready to tackle the problem at hand: how to convince an employer to hire him. He would start, as Jim suggested, with gathering information for a personal data sheet. Jim had explained that a personal data sheet was like a résumé, but more detailed. It should include personal information, like his social security number, so that he could use it to fill out job applications without having to remember all the details of his life every time he filled out an application. Once he had his personal data sheet, he would use it to fill out his first, real application and set a time with Jim to do a practice interview. That would be the real test of whether he had been paying attention in class.

His buddy, Chas, had already told Jim he wanted to be the first one interviewed in front of the class. Chas was working on an application in class today that he had picked up on the way into class. Jason thought Chas was "jumping the gun" since the job application he had picked up was to work in one of those quick oil change places. Chas could barely bend over to pick up something that fell on the floor today in class because of his bad back. How was he going to convince an employer that he could lean over a car engine for any length of time? Oh well, tomorrow's interview with Jim would give him a chance to try his luck in a safe place—class.

DEVELOPING JOB SEEKING SKILLS

The job seeking skills component of placement readiness involves learning

- How to find job openings
- How to develop a résumé, personal data sheet, qualifications brief, or vita
- How to secure and complete applications
- How to set up an interview appointment
- How to interview successfully
- How to follow up on job leads

Job seeking skills training typically makes up the bulk of instructional activities undertaken in placement readiness programs. Indeed, job seeking skills are essential in preparing to enter the world of work. To secure employment, it is often necessary to submit numerous applications, set multiple appointments, and interview repeatedly. With good job seeking skills, clients can often place themselves. In fact, the expectation for informational- and instructional-level clients is that they will self-place. However, without adequate job seeking skills, even these clients will likely require counselor placement or advocacy-level intervention.

Counseling Strategies

A vehicle for introducing job seeking skills content is to use a sales analogy. In Figure 7.1, a sales approach is paralleled with a job seeking approach (see Appendix F for blackline master). Clients need to understand that the work they have done up to this point in self-awareness and vocational selection is part off the pre-approach to job seeking. As they begin work in the job seeking skills area, they are completing the pre-approach stage by putting on paper a job seeking plan from contacts off their job analyses and work they will do in this area. The bulk of the work in the job seeking skills area, however, will constitute the approach stage. In this stage, clients are expected to develop "advertisements" for themselves, such as résumés, completed applications, or portfolios. They refine their interviewing skills and generate answers to the difficult questions interviewers will have for and about them. The final stage in the sales approach to job seeking is follow-up, and clients need to understand that recontacting prospective employers is their responsibility—the "sale" is a job offer.

Job seeking skills can be explored initially with most clients in a group process. What employers are looking for regarding applications, résumés, and interviews can easily be discussed in large and/or small groups. Likewise, discussions surrounding the most effective job seeking strategies and most common errors people make in their job seeking efforts lend themselves to the group counseling format.

Comparing a variety of fictitious applicants, in a group meeting, can be helpful. The facilitator can bring in a series of application samples or show a series of individuals interviewing on videotape. Group members then discuss what they liked or did not like about the "applicants" as they appeared on paper or film. Sometimes a group member will have had a similar experience and can discuss with the group what he or she might have done differently.

However, the implementation of job seeking skills can best be monitored and facilitated on an individual basis. Helping a client develop a personal data sheet, a résumé, or an application demands individual attention. An example of a personal data worksheet is provided in Figure 7.2 (see Appendix F for blackline master). Likewise, refining an interview style may well require one-to-one involvement. The following sections detail activities designed to enhance job seeking skills.

Job Seeking Strategies

Wegmann, Chapman, and Johnson (1985) identified three levels of job seeking strategies, which they identified as A, B, and C levels. Persons using intermediaries (e.g., employment agency personnel, classified advertising, counselor leads—*anyone* other than the job seeker or *anything on paper* between the job seeker and the job) are identified as using C-level job seeking strategies. The results of such endeavors are typically C-level jobs: mediocre, with high turnover rates, minimal salary, limited opportunity for growth, and frequently no benefits.

A Sales Approach to Job Seeking

Stage	Sales		Job Seeking	
	Activity		Activity	Result
Pre-Approach	Product awareness and analysis		Client self-awareness	Awareness of employment strengths and weaknesses
	Customer need awareness and analysis		Job market assessment	Awareness of job requirements and types of jobs available
	Plan of contacts		Job seeking plan	List of places to consider
Approach	Advertising		Telephone contact, letter of intent, application, résumé or vita	Appointments for interviews or other job leads
	Product Presentation		Presenting worker qualifications, relate skills to job duties, answer questions	Get job or not
	Answering objections		Acknowledge objections, supply information to counteract objections	Get job or not
Closing	Making the sale		Get commitment for job, find out next step in process	Get job or make plans for follow-up
Follow-up	Recontacting on a regular schedule		Call back to express interest or find out about other jobs	Keep active and keep employment doors open

Figure 7.1. A Sales Approach to Job Seeking.

Personal Data Sheet

Name (First, Middle, Last)
Address (Street, City, State, Zip Code)
Phone (Include area code)
Social Security Number

Educational Experience:

School(s)
Location
Dates attended
Diplomas, degrees, or certificates received

Work History:

Company(ies)
Location
Supervisor
Dates of employment
Starting salary and ending salary
Job title and duties

Special Skills:

(Computer skills, software use—word processing, spreadsheets, databases; foreign languages
(verbal and written skills); writing skills (grants, reports, creative efforts); skills requiring licensure
(medical, physical or occupational or speech therapy, social work, teaching, counseling);
athletic performance or artistic efforts; compensatory skills, if appropriate for job; ability to
use hand tools and/or power tools; ability to drive or operate equipment; etc.)

Other Related Experience:

(Volunteer work, membership in school or extracurricular groups, etc.)

References: (This can be on a separate page, if necessary.)

Name, Address, Phone (work phone and fax, or home phone)
(Include three or four nonpersonal references)

Figure 7.2. Personal Data Sheet.

Cold calls (sales jargon for calling on customers one has never encountered previously) are identified as B-level strategies. The self-initiative required to perform cold calls to potential employers is repaid in the higher quality of jobs obtained. For the most part, jobs secured in this manner are not advertised to the general public. Jobs obtained through B-level strategies typically pay better and offer more benefits, stability, advancement opportunity, and likelihood to accommodate individual differences than C-level jobs.

A-level job seeking is contingent upon being known by someone working for the company where one wishes to be employed. Simply, it boils down to *whom*—the people—an individual knows. A-level jobs are the most advantageous. Salaries in A-level jobs are very competitive and benefit packages are lucrative. Some of the many benefits include travel allowances, generous vacation and sick leave policies, opportunities for advancement, and environmental amenities.

In a recent study conducted by the Center on Promoting Employment (Fesko & Temelini, in press), the critical importance of networking to obtain job leads for people with disabilities was affirmed. When the networking approach was compared with other strategies (reviewing classified ads, attending job fairs, etc.), networking was found to be most effective. Using the networking strategy typically resulted in higher hourly wages, a greater number of hours worked, and a shorter time spent searching for a job. Counselors must encourage clients to develop and use the networking approach as a primary tool in their job seeking efforts.

Writing Activities

The development of résumés and related writing tasks lends itself to individual instruction. Résumés, qualifications briefs, vitae, and personal data sheets are basically paperwork variations containing career-relevant information. They are used to substantiate related work histories, special talents that might be missed by standard applications, outstanding contributions, awards, and so on. An individual with limited paid work experience may choose to develop a qualifications brief rather than a formal résumé. A qualifications brief would allow such a person to focus on skills developed in school or leisure activities rather than specific on-the-job training and experiences. An example of a skills brief is included in Appendix C as Handout C.1. Individuals with extensive work experiences, accomplishments, and a desire to communicate with a prospective employer about career goals may choose a résumé or vita. The résumé or vita format allows for broader coverage of educational, personal, and vocational areas. If an individual does not have enough information to fill a page, then a résumé is inappropriate; however, such an individual may want to capture pertinent information on paper for future inclusion on a résumé.

Applications

Before filling out applications, if possible, the job candidate should get a job description from the company where he or she wants to apply. By doing so, the client can use the same words on the application as those given in the job description, to match up on paper with the job opening. If the job candidate cannot complete paperwork independently, he or she should prepare, with assistance, a personal data sheet (a print version of all the pertinent data for another to assist with applications, as described in detail in the next section). Counselors should encourage clients, even those who can complete forms independently, to use something like a personal data sheet or a copy of an application filled out previously, for consistency.

Clients should be encouraged to copy their applications both for future reference and in case a company will allow individuals to apply for multiple openings. Some companies allow individuals to use the same completed application form repeatedly, as long as they copy the original without a signature and date, and then sign and date each copy as an "original." If unclear about a personnel office's policy, the client or counselor should ask for clarification.

Counselors need to be aware of current personnel policies. Certain inquiries are unacceptable and illegal on applications, such as the following:

- Do you have a disability?
- What is your marital status?
- What is your native language?
- Have you ever been arrested?

However, similar questions are acceptable and legal, such as the following:

- Do you have any physical impairment that may limit your ability to perform this job? If yes, what can be done to accommodate your limitation?

- Do you have any relatives working for this company? If yes, list names, relation-ships, and city where employed.

- List any languages other than English that you read, write, or speak.

- Have you ever been convicted of a felony? Please explain.

For a more comprehensive listing of fair and unfair preemployment questions, coun-selors may want to consult their state employment (or workforce) commission or state occupational information coordinating committee. There is also a fairly comprehensive listing available as a quick reference in the *Job Seeker's Workbook* (Boerner, 1994a).

Personal Data Sheet

For nonprint readers or individuals with motor difficulties that inhibit their ability to produce well-written applications, the personal data sheet is invaluable. With the per-sonal data sheet, a helper can complete an application for a client without having to rely upon memory for spellings, dates, and such. Advocacy-level clients can also benefit from personal data sheets. Personal data sheets can be laminated for durability (as can other work-related documentation: social security card, alien registration card or proof of citi-zenship, driver's license, etc.). Some clients may also want to carry photos of themselves involved in work or avocational pursuits (e.g., woodworking or performing in front of others) to show evidence of abilities.

Portfolios

For some occupations, a portfolio is required for the individual to be considered a viable candidate. For example, an artist or a jeweler needs a portfolio of his or her creations. Likewise, a photographer, a model, or a writer is required to show work samples. Indi-viduals pursuing careers in the performing arts may be asked to produce demonstration tapes or videotapes and/or be required to audition or produce a portfolio chronicling their careers. Anyone trying to market artistic talents needs a portfolio.

Appointment Setting

Telephone etiquette and appointment setting are good topics for group discussion. A counselor should stress the importance of documenting information obtained by phone, in order to avoid repeated calls or misinformation. Handout C.2 provides guidelines for making calls. Clients also need to understand that they may be asked to set appointments by phone; therefore, scheduling and transportation concerns must have been resolved prior to calling prospective employers. Observation of problems in a client's telephone approach is best handled individually and may necessitate modeling of appropriate behav-ior by the counselor. For example, a counselor may want to have a client call from another office phone and pretend to be making an initial job interview appointment, or the coun-selor may want the client to play the part of a prospective employer and call the client from another office phone to demonstrate how to make the appointment.

Pre-Interviewing

The work involved in preparing for an interview is performed independently by most clients. The research concerning any jobs they might seriously consider applying for should have been completed in the vocational selection process. The crux of what they must do in preparation for job interviews is to develop two critical pieces of information solicited by most job interviewers: a brief personal description and a disability statement.

A brief personal description is exactly as it is called: brief—no more than 2 to 3 minutes (see Handout C.3). It includes a tiny bit of personal information (where a person is from and how long he or she has lived in a particular community). There should be a brief overview of the job seeker's qualifications and skills. The job seeker also may want to share his or her short- and long-term goals, assuming they are relevant. It is essential that the job seeker include a short discussion of work habits and be prepared to respond to queries about them with examples from previous work (or school) efforts. Finally, if the job seeker has talents or interests that relate to the job sought, he or she will also want to share those with the interviewer. It is advisable to write a brief personal description and practice presenting it in preparation for an interview.

For most job seekers with disabilities, it also is important to develop a disability statement. Although the focus of a disability statement is on the positive—what an individual can do—it must also address any preconceived notions the prospective employer has about disabling conditions. For example, if an individual uses a wheelchair to maneuver quickly in a work environment but can walk with the extra support braces offer, he or she needs to explain the different tools for different tasks to an interviewer. Otherwise, an interviewer may falsely assume that the job candidate is unable to walk under any circumstances. Ultimately, the disability statement must allay employer concerns, whether or not those concerns are legitimate. Handout C.4 describes the disability statement process in greater detail.

Interviewing

Interview structure and the consequences of leading the conversation oneself versus following a lead imposed by the interviewer is an excellent topic for group discussion. Likewise, learning how to take the initiative, establishing a friendly rapport, answering open-ended questions, and presenting a functional disability statement are topics amenable to either large or small group situations. In large groups, it can be helpful to solicit volunteers to perform role plays with either each other or the group facilitator and then discuss what has transpired. In small groups, individuals can rotate roles (employer, applicant, observer) and do situational role plays. Interviewer and interviewee rights, including those applicable to all persons and those specific to disabled persons, as well as the pros and cons of filing complaints, can be introduced in a group setting. However, some clients may need to review specifics in a one-to-one setting.

Although actual job interviews are not normally viewed by a client's counselor or fellow group members, videotaped practice interviews can be. Such videotaped viewing can be particularly helpful when a client's effort is critiqued by a group of interested persons. An interview critique form, such as the example in Figure 7.3, is a useful tool for cataloging information from others regarding one's performance (see Appendix F for blackline master). On occasion, job seekers can obtain feedback from an actual job recruiter concerning performance. However, many job recruiters are reluctant to say what their true reasons are for selecting one candidate over another for fear that their comments might be held against them.

As a general rule, clients should be expected to go to job interviews by themselves and perform independently. However, a counselor may go on a job interview with a client when the client is functioning as an advocacy-level client. In fact, a counselor may need to attend and possibly participate in interviews between employers and such

Interview Critique

Name:_____ Date:_____

	Good	Average	Poor
Appearance	☐	☐	☐
Introduction	☐	☐	☐
Establishes friendly interaction with interviewer	☐	☐	☐
Brief personal description	☐	☐	☐
Explanation of disability	☐	☐	☐
Explains work experience as it relates to job	☐	☐	☐
Makes 3 positive statements about self	☐	☐	☐
Pays attention	☐	☐	☐
Ability to answer questions	☐	☐	☐
Ability to ask job-related questions	☐	☐	☐
Understands job duties	☐	☐	☐
Knows about company	☐	☐	☐
Body language	☐	☐	☐
Motivation	☐	☐	☐
Interest	☐	☐	☐
Seems competent/able to sell self	☐	☐	☐
Knows next step in hiring process	☐	☐	☐

Comments: _____

_____

_____

_____

_____

_____

_____

_____

_____

_____

Figure 7.3. Interview Critique.

clients. A counselor may need to clarify to a prospective employer how an advocacy-level client will be able to perform the job duties required. If supported employment strategies, such as job coaching, are to be used, the counselor needs to explain them in detail to a prospective employer. Additional ideas for working with advocacy-level clients are shared in Chapter 12. For informational- and instructional-level clients, an interviewing tip sheet is included as Figure 7.4.

Follow-up

Discussion of follow-up strategies is easily accomplished in either group or individual sessions. It is important for job seekers to understand that, although they are encouraged to check back with prospective employers, they must limit their calls to once a week, unless instructed by the employer to do so more often. If they have been told not to call or come back for a period of time, they must respect the employer's wishes. If a job seeker has had a particularly pleasant interview, he should send a note to thank the prospective employer for his or her time and willingness to discuss the job.

Special Issues

It is important to discuss strategies to obtain applications with and without assistance (e.g., calling to ask a company to mail an application). Responsibility issues regarding having someone else fill out job applications need attention and can be handled well in a group discussion. Basically, the application is a direct reflection of the person who has signed as applicant. What an application tells an employer about the applicant in terms of neatness, ability to follow instructions, completeness of information provided, work

---

Tips for Interviewees

- Research the company in advance (call and ask for public information, go to the library, read newspaper, ask people you know who work there about the company, etc.).
- Establish a friendly rapport with the interviewer (smile, shake hands, visit, use the interviewer's name, etc.).
- Be prepared to respond to, "Tell me a little bit about yourself."
- Give at least three good reasons why you should get the job (e.g., "During high school, I had perfect attendance").
- Have at least one job-related question (e.g., "Will you be my immediate supervisor?").
- Have a prepared functional disability statement (any liabilities: transportation, child care, lack of experience, poor work history, criminal record, chronic health problems, physical limitations, inability to read or write).
- Be prepared to respond to interviewer's disability-related questions (evidence of remediation—what you've done to correct the problem—may be necessary; accommodations to do the job).
- Thank your interviewer (by name) for his or her time, and find out the next step in the hiring process (ask if you can check back and if so, when).
- Follow up (thank you note, telephone inquiries, visits) but don't be a pest! If you don't get the job, ask for referrals to other, similar positions. Don't give up!
- Document for your files: where you interviewed, with whom you interviewed, when you interviewed, how and when to check back on your status in the hiring process—write it all down.

Figure 7.4. Tips for interviewees.

history, and more, is a topic also amenable to group discussion sessions. How to address disability questions and problem areas (limited work experience, numerous short-term jobs, firings, criminal records, chronic health problems, etc.) may be discussed generically within the group structure. However, specific areas of client concern often require individualized intervention.

Figure 7.5 details the kinds of interventions a counselor may need to provide at each of the intervention levels, informational, instructional, and advocacy. These client levels are discussed in greater detail in Chapters 10 through 12.

Because job seeking skills are often perceived as the most critical competencies for clients to develop, many resources are available to address these issues. These resources are frequently usable by career counselors in their efforts to assist people with disabilities. In addition, of the content areas, the job seeking skills area is most likely to have been addressed in educational settings. The key to success in this area is practice, practice, practice . . . followed by review! Counselors will do well to ask to see evidence of the accomplishments reported by clients in this area: copies of applications filled out for submission, copies of letters of inquiry, and the like. If counselors have not seen clients perform in interview situations, they should set up role-play situations that enable clients to practice in advance of going out on actual interviews. The job seeking skills area lends itself to practical application and review of materials developed by others (examples of résumés, applications, portfolio materials, letters, etc.).

Job Seeking Skills	**Levels of Intervention**		
	Informational	**Instructional**	**Advocacy**
Job/Self Match	Give information about jobs Assist with self-analysis Monitor selection process	Educate about jobs Educate about self Educate about selection process	Select job goal for client
Job Search	Tell about where to find leads Monitor job search	Educate about job leads Educate about job search process Help select job leads Structure job search	Select what jobs to pursue Arrange interviews
Applications/Résumés	Provide minimal assistance for applications Monitor/review applications Review résumé	Educate about job applications Practice job applications Structure writing of résumés	Complete job applications for client
Interviews	Provide interviewing information Give information about company	Educate about job interviews Practice interviewing Help set up interviews	Accompany to interviews Assist during interviews
Follow-up	Monitor follow-up efforts	Educate about follow-up Structure follow-up	Assist to perform or perform follow-up

Figure 7.5. Counselor interventions categorized by job seeking skills area and level of client capability.

What Jason did . . .

Jim had lots of application blanks available for group members to peruse or pick up. Jason used his personal data sheet to fill out an application for a local restaurant. He didn't plan to work at the restaurant, but wanted to fill out an application for Jim to critique. Having the data sheet made filling out the application much easier than he had expected. With his low vision device, he had been able to complete the form independently.

Once he had filled out the application, Jason decided to write out his personal description and a disability statement. It was not easy! Jim had stressed the need for both to be positive and informative. He wanted the group participants to have prepared statements to practice presenting in their mock interviews and now Jason understood why: If he had tried to present either without preparation, he would have been tongue-tied for sure. After he wrote and rewrote what he wanted to say, Jason decided to tape record what he had written to "hear" himself make the presentation. He practiced on tape for about a half an hour before he was comfortable with what he had prepared. Although the real test would come when Jim did his mock interview, he felt better for having prepared.

Learning Activities

▶ Reading

Visit a local bookstore and browse the self-help section or the business and careers section to become familiar with the books available for today's job seeker. You will find books specific to developing résumés, books devoted to interviewing, and volumes concerned with where jobs are locally, nationally, and internationally. There will be books describing jobs in the public and private sectors, books about working at temporary jobs, and volumes geared specifically to women or minorities. Hundreds of books are published each year about what is going on in the labor market and how to get into it. As a counselor, it is not as important to have multiple volumes on each topic as it is to know what is available. If you see something that you think is particularly helpful (e.g., a book on becoming a writer and you have worked with numerous clients who have expressed interest in that area), by all means add it to your personal library or make a note of the author and title and check it out from the public library for review. Although few books deal specifically with job seeking skills for people with disabilities, many of the concepts included in the books for job seekers without disabilities are relevant to individuals with disabilities. As you browse, you may want to cross-reference the materials you find with materials included in the Recommended Readings later in this book for future reference.

▶ Doing

Take time to write out what you will say the next time a prospective employer asks you to tell a little bit about yourself. What will you share about your personal life, work experiences, educational accomplishments, special talents, and goals. Write 2 to 3 minutes worth of information. You may want to consider tape-recording what you have written and listening to what you have said. What would you think if you were the boss and meeting you for the first time? Once you have satisfactorily written this introduction to yourself, write the other major points you will need to cover in your prospective interview. You will want to capture on paper three good reasons why you should get the job, at least one job-related question, and your disability statement with a description of what you will do to either remediate or compensate for problems.

CHAPTER 8

Job Maintenance Skills

Jason thought back over today's class. It was neat having Tom in the class. Before the accident in which he had been badly burned, Tom had served in the military and then become a truck driver. He had wonderful stories to tell and was eager to share with the group his experiences with employers and coworkers. This morning Jim had started class with a discussion he called "The Perfect Worker." He had asked the participants to say what they would look for in a worker they might hire. All the usual things were listed: someone who could be trusted, was punctual, dressed well (clean and appropriate for the job), performed the job well and without grinching, was friendly but not intrusive, was interested in the job and in coworkers, and so forth. Then Jim had asked, "Is there a bottom-line, something that's more important than any other thing on this list?" and Tom had said, "The perfect worker is someone you could travel across the country with and never worry that you might not get along or be safe." Jason thought that about summed it up.

EXPLORING JOB MAINTENANCE SKILLS

Job maintenance skills are indicated by a person's knowledge of how to keep a job and how to advance in a job. To be successful in this area, an individual needs to have an understanding of employer and coworker expectations. It is also advantageous to consider how expectations change over time. Perhaps the most critical component of job maintenance is the ability to demonstrate good work habits (attendance and punctuality, interpersonal skills, cooperation, and willingness to follow both written and unwritten rules). Inherent in good work habits is the ability to discipline oneself.

Individuals skilled in job maintenance can evaluate personal problems that may result in distractions from work and resolve those issues outside of the job setting. Such individuals also have an adequate understanding of their job benefits, payroll deductions, and related personnel benefits issues. If labor unions are operating in a client's work environment, the client needs to listen to what the union offers and requires to determine whether to join.

In addition, job maintenance may require the ability to adjust to a new work environment or a different location altogether. Likewise, adjusting to changes in supervision, duties, schedules, and other key features of employment may be necessary to keep a job. Economic trends, international and national labor climates, management takeover demands, computer literacy, robotics, and similar issues require workers to develop problem-solving skills and apply them in order to keep their jobs.

Many of the key concepts related to job maintenance—getting along with others, demonstrating appropriate work habits, understanding the work environment (organizational structure, payroll and benefits information, career ladder, personnel evaluation systems, etc.)—can easily be presented in group counseling sessions. Specific issues of concern, such as a participant's tardiness or other work-related problems, require individual attention and follow-through from the counselor or group facilitator. In the sections that follow, some of the major content clients need to learn related to job maintenance is presented chronologically, from the first day on the job through the first year.

Employer Expectations

First Day and First Week

From the beginning, employees are expected to be on time. If an individual is not sure how long it will take to travel to and from work, a trial run should be arranged in advance of starting at approximately the same time he or she anticipates traveling henceforth. Likewise, new employees are expected to dress appropriately and be well groomed. Hopefully, a new employee has a required uniform or is familiar with a dress code as discussed in the preemployment interview. If a new worker has any question about dress code, he or she needs to call in advance and find out what the expectation is. Although new employees are not expected to recognize and remember the full names of all the people they meet in the first week of work, it is important to make an effort to be pleasant and to remember as many names as possible, especially the names of the coworkers in one's immediate area and the supervisory staff. New employees should expect to be supervised closely at first as they learn and develop skills specific to their jobs. They must listen closely to instructions or read instructions thoroughly and pay close attention to corrections. It is expected that new employees will ask questions, if there is something they do not understand. During the first week, a worker establishes his or her work reputation. By working hard and being productive, a worker makes a good first impression. This is critical because first impressions are difficult to change.

First Month

Employees are expected to be at work and to be punctual because others are depending on them. They are expected to take only the lunch time and break times allowed and to do so at the specified times. They are expected to know written and unwritten company policies. By the end of the first month, new employees should know the majority of their coworkers and the supervisory staff. They are expected to know about informal structures (cliques) and how to fit in at work. New employees should resist the temptation to gossip or take rumors seriously.

Within the first month, new employees are expected to become acclimated to their environment—to know where to go for what and to whom to go for what. They are expected to show an increase in their production and a decrease in the amount of supervision needed. It is anticipated that they will know their own job responsibilities and a little bit about the job responsibilities of others. Finally, it is important to determine the company's policy regarding performance evaluations and probationary periods within the first month in order to begin preparation for same.

Six Months to One Year

After 6 months to 1 year of employment, primary job responsibilities should be second nature. The worker should be able to complete his or her own job and assist newly hired workers. The worker should be self-directed and able to find productive things to do even in slack times; be willing to expand work skills through off-the-job training (in company-sponsored training classes or courses offered in the community); be demonstrating commitment to the company through active involvement in company-sponsored events or community projects; and be diligent (no long weekends) and wary of developing a false sense of security (because if the company does not perform well, employees—even good ones—may find themselves laid off).

It is important for counselors to discuss with clients how relationships and expectations change over time. In particular, it is important for prospective workers to understand how the employer's expectations will change over time. An employer's expectations of workers who are new are much more lenient than expectations at 6 months or a year. (See Handout D.1 in Appendix D for a detailed listing of how employers' expectations change over time.) Likewise, coworkers' expectations of a peer change after a "break-in" period. Most coworkers expect to help new-hires "learn the ropes" and become acquainted with the workplace. Although they usually do not mind if someone new to the office asks for help or clarification, they soon tire of being asked the same question over and over or being relied upon to do another worker's problem solving repeatedly. Within a reasonable period of time, usually 3 to 6 months, employees are expected by supervisors and coworkers to be able to function fairly independently.

Work Habits

All workers are expected to demonstrate certain work habits: being at work (attendance), being on time to work (punctuality), working hard (productivity), getting started without prodding (initiative), getting along with others (interpersonal skills), working well with others (cooperation), working without making errors (quality control), following work rules and regulations (responsibility), being able to do more than one job or component of a task (flexibility), improving job performance over time, presenting an appropriate appearance, and accepting constructive criticism. An excellent way for the counselor to introduce these ideas is to ask clients to generate a list of the qualities they think are demonstrated by a "perfect worker." The list should include the work behaviors listed at the beginning of this paragraph. If the clients leave any of the behaviors off the list, the counselor can add them. Once the perfect worker list has been produced, clients can compare themselves to the ideal worker. On a separate sheet of paper (or on tape for nonwriters), each client should describe how he or she is like or not like the perfect worker. These listings provide two important pieces of information: (a) positive attributes that a client can share ultimately in job interviews and (b) areas in need of improvement that a client can use to set goals. Job maintenance is contingent upon well-developed work habits, and exploring what it takes to be a perfect worker helps clients comprehend their strengths and weaknesses in this area.

Problem Solving

Once clients have identified areas of concern related to job maintenance, they must develop plans to rectify problem areas. A viable approach is the problem-solving model, articulated by Carkhuff (1969, 1993), which is presented in the following paragraphs with suggested counselor interventions.

The first stage of the problem-solving model is *self-exploration*. During this stage the client has to mull over what problem he or she is facing. What is interfering with his or her plans or relationships? What is upsetting or bothersome? The client must identify what problem he or she is wrestling with and be willing to effect change to improve the situation. Throughout the client's self-exploration, the counselor's role is to be an active listener. It is critical that the counselor not jump into a client's exploration with suggestions as to what the counselor thinks the problem is or what the counselor thinks the client needs to do. The objective at this stage is for the client to identify the problem.

The second stage of the problem-solving model is *understanding*. During this stage the client must analyze his or her current situation and determine what circumstances are contributing to the problem and who is contributing to the problem. The client must answer four questions:

1. How am I contributing to this problem?

2. How are others contributing to this problem?

3. How does the environment contribute to this problem?

4. What has kept me from solving this problem?

During the understanding stage, the counselor's role is that of information sharer. Therefore, if a client does not address the previously listed questions, the counselor may want to ask the questions of the client. Once the client has understood the ramifications of the problem, he or she should be able to say what the alternative to the problem is. The alternative to the problem is its solution—a goal. When the client identifies the goal, the counselor helps generate a list of activities the client might undertake to achieve the goal through brainstorming or information sharing.

The objective in the understanding stage is for the client to develop a plan to achieve his or her goal, in other words, to solve the problem. By using brainstorming (sharing ideas without judging them or evaluating them), the counselor helps the client understand his or her array of choices. When it comes time to set a plan down on paper, the following tips are worth sharing with clients:

- Evaluate all the ideas generated (by client, counselor, significant others) and eliminate any that are unrealistic, too expensive, too weird, or "undoable."

- Rank order the ideas from easiest to hardest to do.

- Set the plan on paper with the easiest things to do listed first.

- Always identify a start date and an anticipated date of completion.

- Always identify significant others with whom you will share your plan.

- Always state clearly the goal you are working toward.

- Work on only one step in the plan at a time, in the order set.

The final stage in the problem-solving model is *action*. Once the client has established a plan, it is time to act—to do what needs to be done. One of two things will happen at this point: The client will begin to methodically work on the plan to achieve his or her goal or the client will remain inactive. In both instances, there are things the counselor needs to do to facilitate problem solving. If the client does initiate action, the counselor needs to provide positive feedback or strokes to let the client know that his or her actions are not going unnoticed. If the client does not initiate, the counselor needs to confront the client in an empathetic manner. It is important that the client realize that someone else (the counselor) is aware of his or her plan and expects action. If inaction continues, it will be necessary to recycle through the model: explore (identify the problem), understand (set a plan), and act (initiate the plan). A simplified breakdown of the stages of the problem-solving model and the counselor's role at each stage is presented in Figure 8.1.

Evaluation by Others

Most employers require workers to be evaluated periodically. Personnel evaluations serve multiple purposes: to reinforce good work habits and production, to identify areas in need of improvement, to help workers understand how they compare to their coworkers, and to establish objective criteria for advancement. A counselor running a career counseling or job readiness session can use the group structure to represent a work structure. This enables the group facilitator to solicit feedback from group members regarding each participant's work performance. One activity to promote this idea is to have each group member anonymously complete a Worker Evaluation Form (see Handout D.2 in Appendix D) for each other group member, including the facilitator. The completed evaluation forms are then collected and handed off to an objective third party (e.g., a clerk or secretary to the facilitator), who compiles the responses onto one evaluation form. The composite evaluation forms are returned to group members and reviewed either in the group for feedback from participants or individually between the counselor/facilitator and client. The anonymity of this activity can result in some fairly realistic and objective job maintenance feedback for group participants.

Another group activity to elicit feedback is the "person-out-of-the-room" activity. Although it is called the "person-out-of-the-room" activity, participants do not literally leave the room. They leave figuratively. One at a time, a participant turns his or her back to the group while group members discuss what they like about their colleague and/or what they think needs improvement. The person "out-of-the-room" can hear, but cannot

Simplified Problem-Solving Model	
Client/Student	**Counselor/Teacher**
Self-Exploration (outcome goal: identify problem)	Active Listening Suggestions: "Tell me how you feel," "Help me understand what's wrong," "I hear you saying . . . ," "Sounds like . . . ."
Understanding (outcome goal: develop plan)	Information Sharing Suggestions: "How are you contributing . . . ," "How are others contributing . . . ," "How does the environment contribute to the problem?" "What is keeping you from solving the problem?"
Action (outcome goal: implement plan)	(+) Positive Feedback Suggestions: "I see the progress you're making," "I'm proud of your efforts," "Keep up the good work!" (–) Empathetic Confrontation Suggestions: "I'm confused," "I don't see you working on your plan," "Do you need some help?"

Figure 8.1. Simplified problem-solving model.

speak. The facilitator may want to structure the feedback in a way that everyone is required to say something positive about each other person in the group, or the facilitator may want to ask group members to give only critical feedback if they also will suggest ways for the group member to improve. Once the group has had its say, the person rejoins the group and dialogue between group members often ensues.

Finally, the use of role playing is strongly encouraged to facilitate the acquisition of job maintenance skills. Counselors can have prepared index cards with typical work scenarios printed or brailled and work with clients to act out the described situation. In a group setting, participants can discuss the strategies the players used and note what was effective and what was not. In one-on-one counseling sessions, the counselor and client simply discuss what they felt was and was not effective. If a significant issue or incident has occurred, replaying it in private can help a client understand alternatives to the behavior he or she exhibited or a coworker or boss exhibited. In many instances, a negative behavior is perpetuated because a person does not realize what alternatives are available or simply does not understand the effect of his or her behavior on others. In the latter instance, it is important to say how a client's behavior makes the observer (counselor) feel.

For all job seekers, with and without disabilities, job maintenance skills are essential to job keeping and career advancement. If a worker is disliked or others feel uncomfortable with him or her, the job placement is in jeopardy. Social skills—the ability to get along with others and communicate effectively with others—are critical to career success. For many years, employers have identified good work habits and social skills as the most important factors they consider in hiring and promoting workers (Texas Employment Commission, 1983; Wehman, 1992).

Levels of Relating to Others

Social skills are centered upon people relating well to others. Therefore, a critical job maintenance skill for clients to acquire is the understanding of how one relates to different kinds of people at work. For example, a person relates differently to the boss than to a coworker or subordinate. An excellent vehicle for explaining levels of relationships with other people is the onion analogy, shown in Figure 8.2 (see Appendix F for blackline master) and explained in the following counselor presentation.

> Imagine for a moment that you have an onion in hand, pungent, round, and smooth, with parchment-like skin. It is a good onion, one that you could slice for onion rings to go in a sandwich or to be deep fried. Keep the image of this onion in your mind. Now, mentally slice the onion in half and picture how it looks on the inside. It looks much like a target or the rings of a tree: a small circle of onion in the center with circles of ever-increasing size radiating out from the center.
>
> For the purpose of this onion analogy, assume that the onion you have cut has five broad rings. Each ring represents a different level of relating to other people. The outermost ring or layer represents the *public*, all of those people you come into contact with over time who are virtually unknown to you and to whom you are virtually a stranger. People you pass on the street, people who attended the same schools you did but were not in any of your classes, and people who attend church or community events that you attend but with whom you have only cursory contact fall into this category. At this level of relating to others, the expectation is that one will be civil and polite. You might say "hello," but it is unlikely that you would interact at any length with someone who is simply a part of the general public in any more than a perfunctory manner. This level of relationship in no way excuses rude or inconsiderate

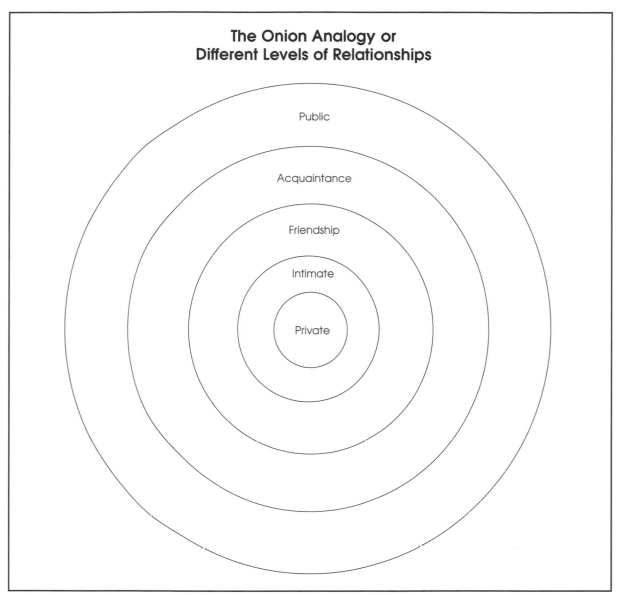

Figure 8.2. The onion analogy or different levels of relationships.   ©1997 by PRO-ED, Inc.

behavior. It is important to attend to others in the environment. If another person is in need, for example, asking directions in an unfamiliar area, it is polite and caring to assist. However, there are situations that warrant caution, particularly when interacting with strangers. Keeping pertinent, confidential information to oneself is called for in public settings.

The next ring in the onion analogy or level of relationships is the *acquaintance* level. At this level are the people whom you know only slightly and who know you only slightly, for example, people with whom you shared classes in school and whose names you learned and who recognize you, and vice versa. Acquaintances are folks with whom you chat about the weather, about seasonal events, and the like (e.g., "Hi. How are you doing?" "Fine. What do you think about this beautiful spring day?").

The third ring is *friendship*. At this level of the onion are friends: those people most like you and most interesting to you, the people you trust with some of your inner thoughts, the people who care about you, the people you care about. Friends are the people with whom you want to converse, sharing ideas, feelings, joys, sorrows. You believe that what a friend tells you is honest. You know that a friend will help out. You know that a friend enjoys being with another friend. People at this level of relating to each other go to movies, go dancing, ride bikes, go to ball games, and dine together. Friendships often last forever. Friends are people to whom you are not afraid to tell your true thoughts. You might approach a friend for a loan or help with transportation. You can discuss politics and religion with friends or avoid those topics, when you know there will be disagreements. The point is you know how your friends feel about certain issues and you either agree or compromise in order to maintain the friendship.

It is important to note at this juncture that, as you move toward the center of the onion, the rings grow smaller. Likewise, as you consider the levels of your relationships, the numbers of people in those respective circles (public, acquaintances, friends) diminish. Although the number of people an individual counts as his or her friends varies from person to person, each person has far more acquaintances than friends and there are far more people in the public than in the acquaintance circle.

The next layer in is known as *intimacy*. Intimates are those few human beings with whom you are closest. For children, intimates are typically family members—mother, father, aunt, uncle, grandmother, grandfather, sister, and/or brother. This relationship does not imply physical intimacy. The concept is broader than merely physical intimacy and includes intellectual and emotional intimacy. Intimates are people you love and trust implicitly. Spouses or significant others are intimates. With partners, there is a combination of physical intimacy, emotional intimacy, and intellectual intimacy. With family members, there is a combination of emotional intimacy and intellectual intimacy. Other significant others who may become intimates, usually intellectual intimates and/or emotional intimates, are priests, rabbis, ministers, and counselors or therapists.

The final layer or ring represents the *private* part of each person. Each person has a private part where information is stored and not shared with anyone else. Here lie the person's most embarrassing moments, wildest fantasies, and most poignant concerns. This notion of having a private part means that no one else knows a person as well as the person knows himself or herself. It is important for each person to feel as if he or she has some secrets or private information that does not need to be shared with anyone. It is healthy to have a private part to oneself, just as it is healthy to have friends, just enough to enjoy and be responsible to over time; to recognize and acknowledge acquaintances; and to attend to those in the general public.

Return for a moment to the onion. Once again picture in your mind the onion, the good onion. Imagine yourself in the store selecting it. You squeeze it to be sure it is firm. If it gives, if it is squishy, you don't choose it. You may even call it to the attention of your grocer, because you know it is not good. If it is squishy, you know it is rotting and that the center is soft. It is an icky onion. Relationships, too, can be healthy or unhealthy, firm or icky. Relationships that develop over time, where two people discover each other's interests, values, abilities, and liabilities and totally accept each other for whom they are, are the kind of relationships that can stand the test of time.

There are two basic personality types—the bleeding heart and the plastic person—that are problematic in terms of building healthy relationships. These are discussed in the following paragraphs. These two personality types will invariably encounter job maintenance problems. When noted, the counselor needs to point out his or her concerns, helping clients to recognize that their behaviors are likely to elicit negative reactions from coworkers and supervisors. If clients recognize themselves in either of these two personality types, they can be reassured that behavior change is possible using the problem-solving model presented earlier in this chapter.

The Bleeding Heart

This personality type is easily recognizable. This is the type of person you may encounter at a bus stop, for example, while waiting patiently for a bus. Someone approaches and says, "Hi." You respond, "Hi. How are you doing?" The other person sighs and sits beside you, "Oh, I'm not doing so well today. My son is having trouble in school. The teacher thinks he's doing drugs and my husband is furious! They had a horrible argument last night and my son threatened to run away from home. My blood pressure and nerves just won't stand much more of this. Every day I say to myself, 'Just leave them. Let them try to fend for themselves; they don't appreciate me,' but I hang in there." Meanwhile, you are praying the bus will come and you can find a seat away from this lady. You don't know her. You don't know how to help her with her problems. You don't understand why she is sharing such personal, private information with you. You feel frustrated and uncomfortable with the extent of this self-revelation from a stranger.

People who are bleeding hearts are often lonely people. They are looking for someone to listen to them and care about them and so they reach out to anyone, anywhere, anytime. They are almost like drowning people, grabbing at anything in sight. They frighten others because they are overwhelming. Their emotional exposés ultimately have the opposite effect from what they want: Others tend to withdraw from them rather than gravitate to them.

The Plastic Person

The plastic person is at the other end of the spectrum from the bleeding heart. Whereas the bleeding heart tells too much, too fast, the plastic person tells too little, too slowly. Although you may have known the plastic person for years, you don't know whether his or her parents are living or dead, where the person lives or what the parents do for a living, whether the person likes sports, what type of music he or she listens to, whether he or she has a girlfriend or a boyfriend, or whether this person has anything in common with you. These individuals are considered aloof or standoffish, and they rarely initiate contact. They usually respond if spoken to, but with no more than an easy answer and no follow-up question in return.

Plastic people, like bleeding hearts, are often lonely people. They do not know how to open up to others to develop relationships. Sometimes they are afraid to say something self-revealing, not realizing that others cannot determine who they really are without shared information. They drive people away by never letting others into their hearts or heads. They may think it is safer to say nothing than to risk another's derision or misunderstanding or jesting or the like.

Before leaving the onion analogy, let me clarify that one does not typically have such tidy boundaries in one's life as presented here in terms of five levels of relationships: public, acquaintances, friendships, intimates, and a private self. Numerous people sit on the cusp of those categories. There are new acquaintances who are almost like the public; acquaintances with whom one has only just begun to develop a friendship; people with whom one may, over time, develop closer relationships; friends who are more like acquaintances than intimates; and friends who are more like intimates than acquaintances. Just as a real onion has many more than five layers, many people have more than five simple categories for people with whom they relate. However, for the purposes of this lesson, the five levels provide an adequate means for categorizing relationships.

· ·

What Jason did . . .

Jason listed his best work habits: good attendance, punctual, good listener, honest, good at following directions, and careful with things such as tools and equipment. He also listed the areas that he thought he might need to improve: too shy to initiate conversations, too quiet sometimes to be noticed, uncomfortable about discussing his visual impairment, awkward around other people, and a worrywart. He thought again about what Tom had said: "The perfect worker is someone you could travel across the country with and never worry that you might not get along or be safe." He decided that another person would feel safe with someone like himself, but he thought it might get tiresome to travel with himself because he wasn't much of a talker. Jason decided to use the problem-solving model to take a look at his problem with initiating conversations.

He felt like he knew what the problem was: too quiet, not a talker. He decided to answer the four questions Jim had suggested as critical to understanding the problem and write out his answers. He wrote:

> How do I contribute to this problem? I feel more comfortable listening than talking. If I don't say anything, people won't notice me and I won't be put on the spot. Sometimes I pretend to be busy with other things (listening to music or reading a magazine) to keep people at bay.

> How do others contribute to this problem? It seems like most people like to talk and talk and talk.... Much of what they talk about doesn't interest me. If they want to know something that I know, they'll usually ask me and I'll answer their questions. My friends and family like me the way I am, and strangers seem to avoid contact with me. It's easy to keep them at bay by just listening and not starting conversations or by pretending to be engrossed in listening to my music.

> How does the environment contribute to this problem? It seems there is an unwritten rule that blind people should be "seen and not heard" as if they don't have much to contribute to the world of sighted people.

> What has kept me from solving this problem? It is easier to listen than to speak and risk saying something odd to others or saying something to the wrong person.

The next thing he planned to do was generate a list of things he could do to solve his problem. From the list of brainstormed ideas, he would develop an action plan. He would share the plan with Jim and Tom and his family, the people who cared about him the most. They certainly wouldn't let him off the hook. They would help him help himself.

Learning Activities

▶ Reading

Read Carkhuff's (1969) *Helping and Human Relations: A Primer for Lay and Professional Helpers,* Volume 2; Carkhuff's (1993) *The Art of Helping VII;* or Ludden's (1992) *Job Savvy: How To Be a Success at Work.*

▶ Doing

Evaluate your own job maintenance skills and then ask at least five other people to evaluate your work performance, using the Worker Evaluation Form included as Handout D.2 in Appendix D. Compare what you think of yourself with what other people said about you. Are there areas where you need to improve? What can you do to make yourself a better worker?

CHAPTER 9

Job Search Skills

Jason was determined to follow through with his plan. This weekend he would continue to prepare for his job search. He would be sure his clothes were ready: He had three pairs of trousers (black, gray, and tan) and five shirts washed and ironed. All the rest of his clothes were clean, and his shoes had been polished. He even had a couple of ties, just in case. He had copies of his personal data sheet and multiple copies of his qualifications brief. He had an appointment book, with two appointments already scheduled. His first appointment was Monday afternoon at a software company to do an informational interview with a game developer. He was very excited about that interview. The guy's name was Gary and he sounded really laid-back. He said to drop by anytime on Monday afternoon. Jason thought 2:00 might be about right—after lunch but not too close to quitting time.

The software company was in the suburbs; to get there he would have to take a bus downtown and transfer. He thought he might get a fairly early start Monday morning, get downtown by around 9:00 or 9:30, and then pick up applications at a sporting goods store and a couple of computer stores downtown. If possible, he would take those applications home to fill out. If the businesses wanted him to fill them out on the spot, he would have enough time to complete at least one or two before lunchtime. He would take a lunch (something simple and not messy) and eat in the park downtown. There was a public washroom where he could clean up and then catch the bus to the software developer's company. He could easily be there by 2:00. He would take his small cassette recorder in his backpack and tape the interview (he had asked Gary, who had said, "No problem").

Tuesday was an open day right now. Jason would try to return any applications he had completed and pick up more, time permitting. Wednesday morning at 9:00 he had an appointment at the community college to do an informational interview with their sound technician at the campus media center. He thought he'd better wear a tie that day. While on campus Wednesday, he thought he would pick up a course schedule and check out the registration process, in case he wanted to take some classes this fall. Late Wednesday afternoon, around 3:30 or 4:00, he and Jim were supposed to meet with Ed, his rehabilitation counselor, to discuss his career plans and what he had gained from the job readiness program. He couldn't wait to share with Ed and Jim what progress he was making. He felt great about the experience.

PUTTING IT ALL TOGETHER: THE JOB SEARCH

The job search area presents an opportunity to put knowledge of job seeking skills to practical use. The necessary skills include organizing time and resources for a job search, negotiating with significant others (mate, parents, counselor) in the development of a career plan, documenting one's efforts, determining when to shift to a backup plan, identifying people who might be able to help find job openings, recognizing appropriate jobs, knowing when to submit completed applications and supporting paperwork, and understanding when and how to follow up after an interview.

To encourage client self-placement whenever possible, counselors may wish to positively reinforce individual efforts. No news is *not* good news when an individual has been steadfastly pursuing work. A counselor's kind encouragement and praise for efforts will likely be welcome. Likewise, monitoring of a client's efforts provides a counselor with valuable feedback regarding the person's level of initiative, follow-through, and need for additional counselor intervention.

Group Interventions

The primary function a group serves during a job search is to monitor each group member's progress. When an active job seeker reports his or her progress to the group, the group can reaffirm the individual's efforts by providing supportive feedback. If a person reports that he or she is discouraged or frustrated, his or her peers can often be a safe "sounding board" and can brainstorm ideas with the job seeker for changing whatever part of the plan is seemingly not working.

An additional advantage to meeting with job seekers in a group is the networking potential. Often, group members will report to the group about opportunities they have uncovered in the community. Providing leads to each other and dialoguing with others about job possibilities are very constructive by-products of the group process. Questions that participants may wish to consider include the following: How realistic *is* this job offer? Are there hidden agendas embedded in a particular job posting (e.g., was the description written for someone within the organization or tailored to a particular individual outside the organization)? Has anyone ever heard of this company? How is the company performing in terms of profits, growth, and stability? Does this company have a reputation for supporting its workers?

Individualized Interventions

Some job seekers need or want individual assistance, sometimes in combination with group activities and other times without. With individual clients, counselors may wish to implement written job search contracts. In such contracts, anticipated counselor and client behaviors are spelled out over a mutually determined time span. If a client states that he or she will make a minimum of three job contacts daily over a period of 2 months and report to the counselor weekly, then both client and counselor have a clear understanding of their responsibilities and expectations of each other. During individual job search activities, documentation is of utmost importance. To avoid redundancy and not rely too heavily on memory, job seekers and their helpers need adequate recorded references to what has transpired and what still needs to be accomplished. A job search checklist, such as that shown in Figure 9.1 (see Appendix F for blackline master), can be of assistance to clients.

Special Issues

Job seekers should be encouraged to keep a calendar. All appointments need to be noted on their calendars. For individuals with visual, cognitive, or motor impairments that

Job Search Checklist

Name:_____ Date: _____

Organize job search time (daily activity)	☐
Identify appropriate job openings (minimum of 4 a day)	☐
Call to solicit job postings for openings identified	☐
Pick up (or have mailed) job applications	☐
Complete job applications	☐
Copy completed job applications	☐
Submit job applications	☐
Find out closing dates for jobs of interest	☐
Call to check application status	☐
Schedule job interviews	☐
Arrange transportation to interview	☐
Prepare for interview (clothes, supporting documentation)	☐
Interview for job	☐
Document job contacts (people, places, things)	☐
Send thank you note, if appropriate	☐
Follow up on job interviews	☐
Other _____	☐
_____	☐

Figure 9.1. Job Search Checklist.   ©1997 by PRO-ED, Inc.

inhibit their ability to write in a reminder book or paper calendar, an electronic calendar or note-taking device is often useful.

Transportation concerns can be critical to success in the job search area. Counselors need to ascertain what travel methods clients are planning to use in their job search efforts. Topics for discussion might include the following:

- Private versus public transportation possibilities and consequences of choosing one over the other (e.g., pros and cons of depending on a relative or friend to drive; using mainline buses or trains; using a paratransit or special transit system; walking; driving; cycling)

- Allowing ample time for bus schedule conflicts or private vehicle breakdowns

- Scheduling far enough in advance to ensure a reservation on a special transit service or with a cab company

- Planning a route in order to visit more than one prospective employer a day and submit applications or solicit information

- Arriving at an appointment independently and on time (especially important for a person with mobility impairment to show a level of independence)

Chasing job leads poses a particular dilemma for someone with a visual impairment who cannot see written notices. Reader services need to be negotiated—by the client if possible—as early as feasible in a job search. Whenever possible, an individual's personal network can be tapped into for assistance. Friends and relatives, however, cannot be relied upon exclusively for long-term assistance as readers and reporters of job leads. Intermediaries, such as counselors, may need to provide assistance also. Occasionally, clients may find helpful company staff who are willing to read postings available to them at personnel offices. Some companies routinely send out postings to applicants who are on file. Some companies provide job opening information that clients can access through telephone job lines or computer. However, only larger private companies and public entities have the resources to man job lines and enter extensive listings into computerized job banks.

Access to phone and word processing services can also be burdensome for some clients. Some rehabilitation facilities and agencies provide phone bank services to their clients. With this kind of assistance, clients without home telephones can make calls to prospective employers. Likewise, some facilities provide clerical support for clients to have résumés copied, letters typed, forms and applications filled out, and telephone messages taken. If such services are unavailable, the client and counselor may wish to negotiate for those services through alternative, community-based resources. When in doubt about where to go for such assistance, it can be helpful to contact a reference librarian at the local public library.

Finally, clients who need further assistance (typically, advocacy-level clients) may require job coaches or trainers to help them with job search skills. In such instances, the trainer may produce an application for a client and accompany the job candidate to the job site. The job coach or trainer may explain to the prospective employer how the client can do the job or be trained on the job and supported by the job coach. With advocacy-level clients, counselor placement is more likely than client placement. (Career counseling with these clients is covered in greater detail in Chapter 12.)

Many clients find it helpful to write out an action plan, such as that shown in Figure 9.2. (A blank copy of the Action Plan Form is included as Handout E.1 in Appendix E.) The action plan details the kinds of activities in which the client and significant others will be involved over the course of the job search. If the client is troublesome or has difficulty with follow through, it can be helpful to copy the action plan for the case folder and for significant others to monitor progress. Counselor follow-up with clients on a regular basis is important due to the discouraging nature of job seeking. In fact, many counselors and related service personnel feel strongly that an ongoing support group can make the difference for clients involved in job searches. Depending on the needs of clients, a support group might meet as often as once a week or as infrequently as once a month. The key is to let clients know that their efforts are noted and to provide encouragement.

The Job Club concept, introduced by Azrin and Besalel (1980) in the mid-1970s, was founded on the notion of providing ongoing assistance to unemployed clients and a structured approach to job seeking. Job Clubs modeled on their work were very popular and continue to be used with disenfranchised job seekers and people long out of the labor market. They encourage a behavioral approach to job seeking by helping clients define in behavioral terms what they need to do in order to secure employment. They also provide external supports, such as telephone banks and space for preparing applications and résumés for clients to use in their job seeking efforts. For counselors willing to monitor clients' progress in job seeking over time, the Job Club model is worth investigating.

Action Plan

Name: _Jason Merriweather_   Date: _9/15/96_

The top 3 kinds of jobs I am looking for are:

1. _Software developer_

2. _Media specialist_

3. _Retail salesclerk_

I plan to look __20__ days for number 1, __20__ days for number 2, and __20__ days for number 3

I will look for job leads in the following ways: _____

1. _I will check with every software development company in town (from Chamber of Commerce directory and telephone book); I will check the placement board at the university; I will ask everyone I talk to about postings they know about; I will check the trade magazines and newsletters._

2. _I will check at the facilities I know that hire media folks (schools, agencies, big companies in town); I will talk to people in those jobs about help they may need or jobs they know of; I will check the Governor's Job Bank on a weekly basis; I will check the newspaper every Sunday._

3. _I will cruise through the major malls in town at least once every other week; I will check the newspaper; I will call stores that have joblines; and I'll ask my friends and relatives to keep their eyes open for postings._

Each day I will make ___6–10___ telephone calls.

Each week I will complete _____10 or more_____ applications.

The first place I am going to look is: _SoftGames, Inc. (My appointment Monday is for information, but while I'm there I will scope out whether they have job openings. If so, I will grab an application and return it later.)_

I think the hardest thing for me will be: _staying motivated!_

I feel that I could use some help with: _job leads, encouragement to keep looking, transportation (I will talk with my family and friends to see if they could help out with some of the running around. If not, I will just have to do the whole thing on the bus—it will mean fewer stops in a day)._

I will need help from the following people: _Mom and Dad (transportation and financial support), counselor (job leads, encouragement, magnifier?), friends (transportation, job leads, encouragement)._

I will be disappointed if I don't:

• find a job in __60__ days

• have at least __4__ interviews in the next week _(2 for information and 2 for real job prospects)_

Comments: _Check with the Governor's Job Bank about accessing their posting from their electronic bulletin board, check with Ed Hanson about getting a current low vision evaluation to find out if a stronger magnifier would help with completing applications and reading the newspaper._

Figure 9.2. Action Plan.

One of the greatest concerns for anyone searching for work is maintaining motivation over time. When Bolles was running the National Career Life Planning Center, he published a newsletter filled with gems for job seekers and their counselors. Unfortunately, the center and the newsletter are now defunct. However, the following ideas from Bolles's (1984) *Newsletter About Life/Work Planning* are worth sharing with individuals engaged in the job search process. In the newsletter, "What To Do When You're Feeling Absolutely STUCK in Your Job-Hunt or Career-Change," Bolles used STUCK as an acronym to help clients recall what to do.

The first thing a job seeker should do when feeling stuck in the job seeking process is get some rest: **S**leep. Often, looking for work is harder than actually going to work for 8 or 9 hours a day. Therefore, it is critical that an active job seeker get plenty of rest (6 to 8 hours—not too much, not too little) in order to stave off depression and lethargy. Second, the job seeker needs to find someone with whom to **T**alk about his or her situation. Sometimes job seekers tire of smiling all the time, being pleasant all the time, and feeling that they are less than okay in comparison with all the people who are working. When a person feels out-of-sorts in his or her job search, it is time to find someone who will listen and provide support without giving advice or badgering the job seeker. Sometimes just talking about the discouragement or frustration helps to keep it in perspective. Not talking about it can lead to negativity or bitterness.

The third thing a stuck job seeker needs is to **U**nderstand the nature of decision making. To make good decisions, a person must gather as much information as possible. With regard to the job search process, this means the job seeker needs to review all the information gathered in the preparation stages—self-awareness, vocational selection, job seeking skills, and job maintenance skills—and rethink all that data. What did the client learn about his or her strengths and weaknesses in comparison to jobs? What are his or her job maintenance assets and liabilities? What information has the client compiled to use in the job seeking process? By taking time to review the data already collected and determining whether some additional information is needed, the client can make decisions based on a better understanding of what the possible outcomes might be. The client can consider what the best- and worst-case scenarios might be, in order to choose the best route to ensure success.

The fourth step to getting unstuck is to **C**ommit. When the client has reviewed and reevaluated all the information collected in the career preparation process, it is time to choose what course he or she will take. Without action, it is impossible to determine if the client is on or off track. Better to choose incorrectly and be able to determine that, than to do nothing and never know if the choices available might have worked.

The final, fifth point Bolles makes for getting unstuck is to **K**now thyself. What he means is that each person knows what best motivates himself or herself and, likewise, what is most likely to impede his or her progress. By identifying what motivates and what impedes, clients can circumvent situations likely to keep them stuck and choose situations that are more likely to lead them to employment. For example, if a client knows that he has difficulty reading maps or following directions and therefore has difficulty finding unfamiliar locations, he would do well to go in advance of a job interview to the location, find the office, and note the best route to return for his interview. On the day of his interview, he would do well to allow extra time to relocate the office. By knowing oneself and knowing the kinds of situations that have been troublesome previously, a person can avert a potential disaster.

In summary, for a job seeker to keep from getting stuck in the job search process or to get unstuck in a frustrating job search, Bolles suggested the following:

Sleep

Talk

Understand

Commit

Know thyself

This simple piece of advice has kept many a job seeker on track.

In addition to the Action Plan Handout (E.1) mentioned earlier in this chapter, numerous other forms can help an individual in the process of a job search. The Career Planning Sheet (Handout E.2) has a client detail the job currently being sought as well as jobs he or she would like to do 2 and 10 years hence. It also encourages the client to consider current problems he or she may encounter in the job search. The Career Plan, Handout E.3, is a simplified version of the previous form that has the client map out his or her long-term objective and the steps (short-term objectives) to accomplish same. The Contact Log form (Handout E.4) is designed to help the job searcher keep up with critical information about what companies he or she has applied to, where they are located, what their telephone numbers are, with whom he or she spoke, and what the outcome of the contact with companies was. Using these forms can help a job seeker stay organized and focused.

. . . .

What Jason did . . .

Jason followed his plan to the letter! He went for the interview he had scheduled on Monday with Gary at the software company. He felt that the interview went well. He was relaxed and comfortable with Gary. He even had a chance to give him three good reasons why he should get such a job. He told him about his visual impairment and answered questions Gary had about how he could see the monitor. He made it clear that his visit was for information seeking, but that as soon as he'd finished his research he would apply if there were openings. He was cautiously optimistic about the possibility of being offered a job. Gary said to check back in a week or so and Jason already had it on his calendar to give him a call next Thursday.

He had picked up the applications he was interested in completing on his way to see Gary. He planned to drop them off on Wednesday on his way to his second infor-mation interview . . . but not before he copied them for future reference. He thought it would be wonderful if Gary offered him a job before the end of the month. The wait-ing is the hardest part, he thought. It helped, however, to have the action plan. It made waiting to talk to Gary go faster because he had other things to do.

Learning Activities

▶ **Reading**

If you can locate Richard Bolles's newsletters from the National Career Life Plan-ning Center, read them. Check first with reference librarians at local universities, public libraries, or rehabilitation agencies to see if they have the newsletters in their collections. If you are unable to locate copies through these sources, check with area career counselors who may have copies in their private libraries. Or contact Bolles directly at P.O. Box 379, Walnut Creek, CA 94597. You may also want to seek out newsletters currently in publication, such as the *Career Opportunities News* published by Garrett Park Press (P.O. Box 190-B, Garrett Park, MD 20896) or local newsletters published by state employment agencies, rehabilitation agencies, or career counseling groups.

► **Doing**

Develop a career action plan for yourself.

Career Counseling for Clients with Differing Abilities

CHAPTER 10

Informational-Level Clients

Mike called Jessica, who was listed in the Yellow Pages under vocational services, to see if she could help him with his career plans. He wasn't sure she would want to work with him since he had lost much of his vision in an accident 6 months before. He hadn't lost enough vision to be considered legally blind, according to the state rehabilitation services people. They had referred him to the general rehabilitation services counselor, but Mike wasn't sure he wanted to go through yet another application process, particularly with someone without expertise in vision problems. A person he met at the School for the Blind had told him about Jessica. She had a private practice and supposedly knew about blindness.

When Jessica answered, Mike introduced himself and explained the situation. He needed to get back to work, but he wasn't sure what he could do without vision. Jessica asked about his vision and he explained that he had lost his left eye in an accident and had diminished sight in his right eye. He could no longer drive. She asked if he could see to read print, and he said he could. Mike asked her if it was true that she had worked with blind people and she assured him that she had. He asked if she could help him find a job. Jessica said that she would be glad to meet with him and find out what he needed and discuss what she could provide to determine if they would be able to work well together. She explained that she didn't charge for the initial contact—it was strictly a time for them to get to know one another and determine whether they wanted to work on his case together. Mike felt better about the situation knowing that he would be under no obligation. He felt even better when she offered to come to his parents' home, where he had been living since the accident. This business of not being able to drive was the worst—how could a man work without having access to a car?

WORKING WITH INFORMATIONAL-LEVEL CLIENTS

Informational-level clients are individuals with minimal needs for intervention from service providers. They are people who know what they want and need but who don't know where to get the information they need to make things happen for them. They are often adventitiously disabled adults. They understand the basic premises behind working. They have a work ethic and often a work history. They simply don't know about adaptations and accommodations for people with disabilities. Or, they are bright and capable young people with disabilities who have grown up in strong, supportive families with high expectations. They have been encouraged to be actively involved in their families and communities. They understand about work and expect to contribute to the larger society through their work efforts. They have acquired academic and functional life skills through school and extracurricular involvement. They simply need information and guidance related to the world of work to get started. Once they have the information they need, they are able to apply what they have learned in their own lives. Their need for assistance or intervention from counselors and other service providers is minimal.

The counselor's role in working with informational-level clients is to discover gaps in their knowledge and to provide structured learning activities to fill in those content gaps. The first stage in the counseling process is the same across all levels of client functioning (informational, instructional, and advocacy): The counselor must establish rapport with the client. This means that the counselor must take time to get to know the client and share with the client how the counselor can facilitate. At this stage, it is important for the counselor to ask the client broad, open-ended questions such as "Can you tell me a little bit about yourself?" rather than specific questions such as "How old are you?" "When did you graduate from high school?" or "What kind of job do you want?" Needless to say, the counselor may have to probe along these more specific lines at some point. However, in the beginning of the relationship, the counselor should let the client take the lead and share what he or she feels is most important.

As a general rule of thumb, it is important for the counselor to pose open-ended questions in the following areas:

- Early life experiences and family history

- Education and training (both formal and informal)

- Work experiences (including routine chores, volunteer work, and paid jobs)

- Health and disability issues (congenital or adventitious impairment, stable or progressive disability, chronic or static health concerns, perceived impact of disability)

- Financial status

- Personality characteristics (self-concept, level of confidence, locus of control, interpersonal skills, willingness to self-disclose)

- Perceived liabilities or problems

- Current interests, abilities, and values

- Overall image (strengths and weaknesses)

Depending on the amount of time the counselor can spend in an initial interview, which typically lasts 1 to 2 hours, only some of the areas listed above can be covered. Hopefully, the client will share openly much of the information the counselor needs to determine whether he or she can provide the guidance needed. If the counselor feels that the client doesn't bring up something critical in this initial discussion, the counselor must probe specifically for this information. The counselor needs to leave enough time to share with the client what the counselor can provide, how he or she can facilitate, what his or her credentials are, and what the fees will be. Also, if the counselor works for an agency rather than as a private practitioner, some agency-required forms may need to be processed in this initial interview period.

If the counselor and client decide to work together, they move into the career counseling process. As discussed earlier in this book, five distinct content areas are pertinent to the career counseling process: self-awareness, vocational exploration, job seeking skills, job maintenance skills, and job search skills. Informational-level clients are usually fairly knowledgeable about themselves. Therefore, a good first homework assignment is for the client to list his or her abilities, interests, values, and liabilities. This assignment will provide the counselor, at the next meeting, with a good indication of the client's writing ability, thought processes, and willingness to follow through with assignments. If the client has numerous spelling errors, or writes illegibly, or demonstrates confusion among the categories (interests, abilities, values, and liabilities), then the counselor will know that the client is at the instructional level rather than the informational level.

In subsequent meetings with an informational-level client, the counselor needs to learn as much as possible about the client: the abilities and interests that are marketable and well developed; the rank order of the client's values; the employment ramifications of the client's values; the client's liabilities and what, if anything, can be done about them; the client's self-perceptions and whether they jive with the perceptions of the counselor and others (e.g., other service providers, family members, significant others).

As early in the career counseling process as possible, the counselor should introduce the informational-level client to Bolles's (1997) *What Color Is Your Parachute?* In this book, Bolles discusses the importance of knowing oneself and the labor market in order to make a good decision about what jobs to pursue. He also presents some excellent suggestions for seeking employment, once a person has decided what job to pursue based on his or her qualifications. Counselors can encourage informational-level clients to read the sections in Bolles's book that are relevant to the content area on which they are working in counseling sessions and be prepared to discuss them as a part of the counseling session. Although Bolles updates his book annually, clients may read an older version as the information has been fairly consistent over time. A copy from the library will serve the purpose for most individuals. Other general resources that may be useful are listed in the Recommended Readings section of this book.

If it is unclear how the client's personality type might be defined in relation to work, the counselor may want to consider introducing an assessment tool such as the *Self-Directed Search* (SDS) by Holland (1994). The SDS (available in print and braille) can be taken easily and effectively by an informational-level client. The SDS is a handy tool for clients as they move from the self-awareness content area into the vocational exploration area. As indicated in its title, the SDS can be completed without counselor intervention. However, the counselor should follow up with clients to discuss the results, which may lead to a meaningful discussion of vocational exploration resources.

Because informational-level clients generally are self-starters and enjoy learning, it is important to provide them with numerous vocational exploration resources. As indicated in Chapter 6, there are three major reference books by the U.S. Department of Labor for gathering general information about careers: the *Dictionary of Occupational Titles* (1991), the *Guide to Occupational Exploration* (1979), and the *Occupational Outlook Handbook* (1994). The counselor should discuss these materials, explain how to use them, and encourage clients to go to the public library (or the state or regional library for the blind and physically handicapped) to use them. The counselor may want to share with clients written descriptions of the coding systems, for current and future reference. Also, if clients have taken the SDS, they should be made aware of the *Dictionary of Holland Occupational Codes* (Gottfredson & Holland, 1989). The counselor also might encourage clients to go through materials in the library or at local bookstores related to career choices of interest to them. Popular books are available on most career areas; topics range from general information about jobs in government to sports or specific information about jobs in particular parts of the country or available through temporary services.

As clients research jobs and career opportunities in written reference materials, it is important that they keep notes and write questions that are left unanswered by the books. They may then pose their questions to the counselor and/or workers in those areas of employment. In fact, when the counselor introduces clients to the vocational exploration area and encourages them to begin their research, the counselor should also describe to them the process of vocational exploration. In brief, the process involves looking at general areas of interest, narrowing down choices to three or four specific jobs to research thoroughly, reading as much as possible about those three or four jobs, developing a list of questions for workers in each of those jobs, and then contacting workers and arranging informational interviews.

The concept of informational interviewing needs to be introduced to clients. Although some clients may have heard of informational interviewing or read about it in books like *What Color Is Your Parachute?* (Bolles, 1997), the counselor should not assume that people know or understand the concept. The counselor and client should spend at least one counseling session discussing and clarifying what informational interviewing means. (This concept was first introduced in this text in Chapter 6.) The following key points should be reviewed with clients:

- An informational interview is strictly for seeking information about a job. It is a research technique, not a job seeking technique.

- When the client requests an informational interview, he or she must be clear that he or she is simply doing research and would like 15 to 20 minutes of the worker's time to discuss job duties, training required to secure employment in the field, types of companies that hire such workers, and the like.

- The client must go to the interview well prepared, with specific questions written out to ask the worker.

- The client should take notes and, if using adaptive equipment (tape recorder, note-taking device, or computer), should expect to explain the function of the device and ask permission to use it.

- Even if offered employment, the client should decline and explain that he or she is simply in the research phase of the career exploration process and that he or she appreciates the offer but must decline at present. (After a reasonable period of time, say 2 or 3 weeks, the client can make contact again as a legitimate job seeker to follow up on the offer.)

- Following an informational interview, it is imperative that the interviewer send a card or note to thank the worker for his or her time and effort during the interview.

Sometimes, clients ask counselors for leads to set up informational interviews; when possible, it is appropriate to supply them. If the counselor has no leads for a client, the two should do some brainstorming to determine where and/or from whom they might capture that information. Suggestions for tracking down leads for informational interviews include the client's personal and business network, the telephone directory (particularly the Yellow Pages), directories of professional organizations available through the Chamber of Commerce or Better Business Bureau, membership organizations listed in the *Occupational Outlook Handbook* (U.S. Department of Labor, 1996) or other reference materials, college and university placement offices, public sector job development agencies such as Private Industry Councils or rehabilitation agencies, and so forth.

It is important for individuals with disabilities, to talk, if at all possible, with workers with similar disabilities doing the jobs of interest. In this way clients can find out about adaptations and accommodations that have proven helpful to others. They also can find out about the receptivity of other workers in particular work environments to individuals with disabilities, specialized training programs, and advancement potential. Numerous membership organizations focus on categorical disability issues. One of the most comprehensive sources for contact information is the *Directory of National Information Sources on Disabilities* (National Institute on Disability and Rehabilitation Research, 1994), available through the U.S. Department of Education. Many of the organizations listed have databases of individuals with specific disabilities who are working and would welcome calls from interested persons. In addition, many of the organizations have local chapters or affiliates where individuals gather in supportive groups for recreation and information sharing. These groups may well produce additional leads and information sources for job seekers.

As clients collect information about jobs in which they are interested, they should compile it in some fashion: in manila folders, in computer files, in accordion files, in envelopes, or whatever. No matter what system the client uses, the key is retrieval: Can the information be recaptured easily for future reference? Once the client has collected all the information he or she can concerning jobs of interest, the next task is to evaluate it all. At a minimum, a summary listing pros and cons for each job researched should be produced. After the client has produced the summary sheets for jobs of interest, he or she should compare each job to his interests, abilities, and values. This, in essence, is the discrepancy analysis, as described in Chapter 6.

Informational-level clients should be able to analyze information about the job demands (from their research) and compare it to themselves to determine how well they match and where there are discrepancies. Once clients have identified the differences or discrepancies between themselves and the jobs they have researched, they must consider the implications. Is it possible to return to school or attend some other training program to remediate a deficit or build skills required to do the job? Can adaptive equipment enable a person to do a particular job duty in a different but efficient and safe manner? Are there compensatory skills an individual can acquire to perform adequately? If something can be done to overcome a discrepancy, the client must determine if he or she is willing and able to do so. If nothing can be done to overcome a discrepancy, the client may determine that the particular job of interest is not viable and that he or she needs to consider other work alternatives.

Following the discrepancy analysis process, an informational-level client should have a fairly clear idea of his or her choices in terms of jobs. Ideally, three or more job choices will be ranked by preference. At this point, the client is ready to move into the job seeking skills content area. The counselor should discuss with the client the following information related to job seeking:

- Where to find job openings in areas of interest
- How to complete paperwork in such a way as to maximize one's chances of being called for an interview
- Whether to disclose one's disability in advance of a job interview
- How to successfully interview for a job
- How and when to address disability-related issues in an interview
- How to negotiate with a prospective employer for accommodations
- When and how to follow up after a job interview

Job Leads

As mentioned in Chapter 7, an individual's personal network (friends, family, business acquaintances, and friends of friends) is the best source of information about job leads. Informational-level clients should be encouraged to generate a list of people they know and people known by people they know. Clients should include names, addresses, phone numbers, and affiliations, as well as the name of each person who provided the name of an unknown individual. Clients should then contact the listed individuals to determine whether they know of job openings and are willing to make a referral for them.

The second alternative for generating job leads is to gather the names of companies in the desired work area from print or human resources and to approach those companies without any kind of introduction or knowledge of whether they have jobs open. This technique is referred to as making "cold calls." The third and final strategy for finding job leads is to use an intermediary, human or otherwise. For example, the classified ads are considered an intermediary because they are between the job seeker and the employer; likewise, an employment agency counselor is an intermediary because he or she is between the job seeker and an employer. Anything or anyone between the job seeker and an employer is considered an intermediary. Of the three, the first (personal contacts) is the most likely to produce good job leads and the third (using intermediaries) is the least effective.

Paperwork

To maximize the chances of a client's paperwork being viewed favorably and leading to his or her selection for an interview, the counselor and client should make sure that the following criteria are met:

- The information on the résumé (if one is required or allowed) and on the application *must* indicate that the applicant is qualified for the job. This can best be accomplished by securing a job description before filling out the paperwork and matching what is required with what is shared on the application.

- If a résumé is submitted, it must conform to what is expected in that line of work. In most instances, a single sheet of plain white, bond paper with black ink is ideal. However, for an advertising position with a company known for its zany advertisements, something bolder might be appropriate. Likewise, if the employer asks for a curriculum vita—that is, a detailed work history with educational background, publications, professional affiliations, and the like—in lieu of an application, the applicant would do well to submit more than one page. If there is any doubt, however, go with the most conservative choice: a single page, black on white.

- If an application is required, the client should read and follow the directions, filling out the application completely and neatly. Information entered on the application should be printed or typed (if allowed) and should jive with what the employer is looking for in an applicant. All information should be accurate and current. If something is requested that does not apply, the client should insert "N/A" for "not applicable." Blanks must be filled in with something, unless it is clearly not expected or required. Clients should be cautioned not to share negative information on the application about previous employers or previous work sites.

- If an application requests information that the client feels is inappropriate or illegal, the client has to decide whether he or she wants to work at such a place and, if so, must provide the information. (Perhaps once the person is hired and has established rapport with coworkers, he or she can suggest that the information solicited may not have been legal or ethical to request and should be reconsidered. This is a difficult decision, however, because (a) such honesty could backfire and cause the employee difficulty with a coworker or supervisor or (b) the employee's efforts could be appreciated if the information was solicited in an innocent or uninformed manner.

- If an individual is compelled to self-reveal on an application about a disability, the person must be prepared to note how he or she will compensate for the disability at work. For example, if an individual notes that she attended a residential school for the deaf, an employer would know that she was deaf without asking specifically. The job applicant would then need to indicate how she would manage on the job without hearing. She might indicate that she uses American Sign Language to communicate with other deaf people, but writes notes to hearing people who are unfamiliar with manual communication.

Disclosure

Individuals with disabilities must make employers aware of their disabling conditions before they are hired, if they want protection under the Americans with Disabilities Act. Informational-level clients must, therefore, be prepared to discuss their disabilities with prospective employers. It can be helpful for the client to write out a disability statement, before an interview, and practice recording it or presenting it to a counselor or other caring individual who will provide honest, nonjudgmental feedback to the client. Although employers are not allowed to ask if an applicant has a disability, they can ask if the applicant has any disabling conditions that would prohibit him or her from performing the duties of the job. A client must be able to answer "no" to be considered as qualified for the job.

Interviewing

As described in Chapter 7, interviewing by informational-level clients is best performed independently. However, before the client goes on interviews, the counselor should help the client to consider the following issues:

- How much and what to say in response to the interviewer's opening statement, "Tell me a little bit about yourself"

- What three positive reasons the client can list as qualifications for the job

- What job-related question(s) the client will pose during the interview

- When and what to say in reference to disability issues and related accommodations that may be required

- How the client will discern the next step in the hiring process and take appropriate steps to follow up with the interviewer

Discussing these issues with the counselor will be sufficient for most informational-level clients; however, some individuals may feel more comfortable going to interviews having practiced what they will say with someone like the counselor, who will provide honest feedback.

Job Search

Most informational-level clients will adhere to guidelines or suggestions offered by the counselor in their job search efforts. The counselor may want to share with clients some of the documentation forms provided in this book (e.g., Figure 9.1 or forms in Appendix E) and encourage their use. Informational-level clients should also be encouraged to use calendars or reminder books to help them keep up with their appointments.

An important topic of discussion is how long a client intends to look for a particular kind of job before shifting gears and looking for something else. It is also important for the counselor to find out from the client what kind of supports or monitoring will be needed to keep him or her moving.

- -

What became of Mike . . .

Mike met with Jessica and discussed his desire to return to work. Jessica asked him about his current medical status, living arrangements, and activities. She also asked him about his previous work, avocational, and educational experiences. Mike felt comfortable with her. She answered his questions about doing things without perfect vision by using adapted tools and compensatory skills. He was relieved to know that he could continue to do woodworking projects, for example, with tactually marked tape measures, auditory levels, and safety jigs for power saws. She gave him the names and contact numbers of companies that specialized in adaptive equipment so he could request catalogs.

Jessica explained that she could help him find a job, but that he would do the bulk of the "leg work." She explained that she would share information and resources with him; help him understand how to analyze his interests, abilities, values, and liabilities; and learn about the labor market through activities and assignments. She said she felt that he would be able to do the assignments independently, but would help him if necessary. Mike told her he was willing to give it a try. Jessica gave him his first assignment: Write out 10 interests (any interests—vocational or avocational), 10 abilities (what both he and others felt he was good at doing), his 10 highest values (good thing she gave him that values word list!), and 3 problems or liabilities related to finding work now. He was to bring the completed assignment to their next meeting a week from today.

Learning Activities

▶ Reading

Go to a library or local bookstore and find books, magazines, or journals that provide information related to career decision making. *National Business Employment Weekly*'s (December 29, 1996–January 4, 1997) Job Search & Career Guidance National Best Sellers list follows:[1]

1. *What Color Is Your Parachute?* (1997 edition) by Richard Bolles (Ten Speed Press, Berkeley, CA)

2. *Do What You Are* by Barbara and Paul Tieger (Little, Brown & Co., Boston)

---

[1]*Source:* Barnes & Noble, Inc.'s, survey of job-search and career-guidance book sales in Barnes & Noble, B. Dalton Bookseller, Bookstop, Bookstar, Doubleday, and Scribners bookstores nationwide conducted exclusively for the *National Business Employment Weekly.* Reprinted by permission from the *National Business Employment Weekly,* copyright 1996, Dow Jones & Co., Inc. All rights reserved. For subscription information, call 1-800-JOB-HUNT.

3. *Resumes That Knock 'Em Dead* by Martin Yate (Adams Publications, Holbrook, MA)

4. *Cover Letters That Knock 'Em Dead* by Martin Yate (Adams Publications, Holbrook, MA)

5. *Job Interviews for Dummies* by Joyce Lain Kennedy (IDG Books, San Mateo, CA)

6. *Resumes for Dummies* by Joyce Lain Kennedy (IDG Books, San Mateo, CA)

7. *Love Your Work and Success Will Follow* by Arlene S. Hirsch (John Wiley & Sons, New York)

8. *Knock 'Em Dead '97* by Martin Yate (Adams Publications, Holbrook, MA)

9. *101 Great Answers to Toughest Interview Questions* by Ronald Fry (Career Press, Hawthorne, NJ)

10. *The Quick Resume and Cover Letter Book* by J. Michael Farr (JIST Works, Inc., Indianapolis)

11. *Rites of Passage at $100,000+* (Revised) by John Lucht (Henry Holt, New York)

12. *The Complete Q&A Job Interview Book* by Jeffery Allen (John Wiley & Sons, New York)

13. *Adams Cover Letter Almanac* (Adams Publications, Holbrook, MA)

14. *Discover What You're Best At* by Barry and Linda Gale (Simon & Schuster, New York)

15. *175 High Impact Cover Letters* by Richard Beatty (John Wiley & Sons, New York)

► **Doing**

Prepare a lesson or activity to teach an informational-level client about (a) job interviewing, (b) networking, or (c) making a disability statement. Use resources from this text and from local libraries, rehabilitation or education agencies, and/or career counselors.

CHAPTER 11

Instructional-Level Clients

Juanita went to see her rehabilitation counselor with whom she had worked since high school to ask for help. She really wanted to work, but not at the fast food restaurant where she had worked when she was in high school because it was the only job she and her vocational teacher could think of where Juanita wouldn't have to do a lot of reading and writing. Her learning disability had caused her lots of trouble in school, and many people assumed she couldn't learn. She could—it just took her a little longer, but she wouldn't give up!

When she met with the rehabilitation counselor, Katherine Nelson, Katherine had suggested the Job Readiness Program at Goodwill Industries. The program sounded okay to Juanita once she found out that it didn't mean she would have to work in a sheltered workshop. In fact, it seemed like a really good idea after they talked about what she would learn: how to select a good job, how to apply for jobs, how to interview, and how to keep a job. When she found out that one of the instructors was a woman named Olga Cantu, Juanita was really pleased to think there might be a teacher with a cultural background similar to hers. She thought that maybe Ms. Cantu could help her with some of the spellings of English words that seemed so weird. Juanita told Katherine that she would like to meet with the Goodwill staff.

On the day of her appointment, Juanita took the bus. She arrived about 10 minutes early for her 2:00 P.M. appointment. She checked in with the receptionist, who told her that Don Martin would be with her shortly (she had hoped to visit with Olga!). As she waited, she thought about how excited she was to be getting on with her life. She was 22 years old—it was time to be settled and not have to depend on her parents for support!

Juanita liked Don but found him a bit intimidating. He was very handsome and he talked fast. He explained the program rules: Participants were expected to be present every day, on time and ready to work; they were expected to work cooperatively and participate in all the classroom activities; they would receive only the help they needed; if they had to miss a day or were going to be late, they had to call in; if they missed 3 days they would be dismissed. He told her about the schedule: 8:30 A.M. to 3:30 P.M., Monday through Friday. He said the instructors arrived by 8:00 A.M. and didn't leave until 5:00 P.M., so if she needed additional help she should let one of them know and they would schedule time for her. He didn't seem at all worried about her ability to keep up when she told him about her learning disability. He said there would be other people in the class with similar problems. He thought the group of participants would include about eight men and four women.

Finally, he told her about the other staff members: Sandy and Olga, who were both full-time interns from a rehabilitation program at the local university, would be there every day. Don was the full-time Goodwill instructor, and a woman named Pam Smith was the program director at Goodwill. Pam would do guest lectures and help with some individual career counseling, but Don would be in charge of the day-to-day activities. He asked Juanita if she had any questions, but she was too overwhelmed to think of a thing. He said he would expect her on the following Monday, unless he heard from her otherwise, and then he was gone.

WORKING WITH INSTRUCTIONAL-LEVEL CLIENTS

Instructional-level clients are individuals who need an average amount of intervention from service providers. They need to be taught how to analyze themselves and the job market to choose a career path that makes sense for them. They need to be taught how to fill out applications and develop résumés. They need to practice performing in interview situations. Simply being handed materials to read and being given verbal or written instructions, as can be done for informational-level clients, would overwhelm them and result in very little follow through. These clients might be poor readers or need to "do" or "see" things in order to learn.

The majority of clients in the rehabilitation system, the majority of students in schools, and the majority of the population are instructional-level people—they are average. They need instruction for a limited period of time; however, once they have mastered content or tasks, they can apply what they have learned to their lives. They do not need service providers forever. They graduate, in a sense, and go on about their lives—they work, establish families, and contribute to the community. They may be individuals with congenital or adventitious impairments. Typically, they are of average intelligence and their disabilities tend to be mild or moderate rather than severe or profound impairments.

The counselor's role in working with instructional-level clients is to either provide the direction they need or contract with a community-based service provider or an agency-based rehabilitation center for same. Many of these clients have come through the public school systems and graduated with average academic skills; others have graduated from colleges and universities with average academic skills. The common thread is that they do not know what they want to do vocationally and/or how to successfully get and keep a job.

As with the informational-level clients, the first stage in the counseling process is to establish rapport with the client. The same broad, open-ended questions such as "Can you tell me a little bit about yourself?" are appropriate with instructional- as with informational-level clients. However, if a client is not as forthcoming as desired, the counselor may need to probe with follow-up questions that are more specific. An example follows:

COUNSELOR: Tell me a little bit about yourself.

CLIENT: Well what do you want to know? I'm 20 years old and I injured my back working construction. I need you to help me figure out what I can do now.

COUNSELOR: Share with me about what you did before you injured your back—where you went to school and what you studied.

CLIENT: I graduated from Westwood High School. I didn't like school much—it was boring. I started working construction with my stepfather during my junior year and just stayed with it after high school.

COUNSELOR: I understand. You mentioned working with your stepfather—tell me a little bit about your family.

CLIENT: It's just my mom, me, my stepfather, and my younger brother.

COUNSELOR: Do you live with them or have your own place?

CLIENT: I had to move back in with them when I hurt my back because I couldn't make rent on my place.

COUNSELOR: So you had your own place, but now you are living with your mom, your stepfather, and your younger brother?

CLIENT: Yeah.

COUNSELOR: I see. You also mentioned graduating from Westwood High School. You said you didn't like it much. Will you tell me a bit more about your experiences there—what you liked and didn't like, that sort of thing?

CLIENT: That's easy. I liked sports. I played baseball. I was pretty good—made junior varsity, but I never made varsity. The rest of it was a drag. I couldn't wait to get out and start making some money. I thought I was going to do construction forever—what a bummer! My folks think I need to go back to school. Why? I hated high school. I hated sitting all day and listening to those teachers talk about stuff that I knew I'd never use. Is that my only choice?

As in the example, follow-up probes should be as open ended as possible; otherwise, clients tend to answer simply "yes" or "no." Basically, the counselor should follow the same pattern for soliciting information that was presented in the previous chapter, asking open-ended questions and probing in the following areas:

- Early life experiences and family history

- Education and training (both formal and informal)

- Work experiences (including routine chores, volunteer work, and paid jobs)

- Health and disability issues (congenital or adventitious impairment, stable or progressive disability, chronic or static health concerns, perceived impact of disability)

- Financial status

- Personality characteristics (self-concept, level of confidence, locus of control, interpersonal skills, willingness to self-disclose)

- Perceived liabilities or problems

- Current interests, abilities, and values

- Overall image (strengths and weaknesses)

Once the counselor has established rapport and determined that the client is an instructional-level client, it is important to decide whether the counselor can meet the client's needs through individual instruction and counseling or whether the client's needs can be best met through a classroom instructional approach. To help differentiate between informational- and instructional-level clients, the techniques described in this chapter focus on group counseling and instruction for instructional-level clients. However, a counselor with the time and flexibility can provide individual instruction and counseling using these same techniques. Please note, also, that the techniques described in the previous chapter on informational-level clients may well be appropriate for instructional-level clients. The activities described below are intended as supplementary or additional support activities designed to reinforce the learning process for instructional-level clients.

Self-Awareness Activities

Rather than simply asking clients to write down their interests, abilities, values, and liabilities, the counselor may need to provide them with examples and descriptions of how they can determine these characteristics. If working with a group of instructional-level clients, the counselor could facilitate a discussion of interests within the group membership. The counselor might solicit group members' interests and note them on a chalkboard or overhead projector. The counselor may need to initiate the discussion with examples of a few of his or her own interests. After a substantial number of interests are listed, the counselor should discuss with the group whether all the things listed are shared interests or whether some of the group members might perceive some of the things listed as work or chores. This discussion will help clarify that people's interests vary and differentiation is to be expected. It can also help to have clients think about the skills that they use to perform or participate in the things they enjoy doing (their interests).

Likewise, the counselor can work with clients to generate a listing of various abilities for discussion. The following are some questions the counselor can pose to encourage clients to think broadly about their abilities: "If I were to ask your mother [father, teachers, neighbors, friends, others] what you were good at doing, what would she [he, they] say?" "In what classes did you make the best grades?" "Do you excel in any sports, playing an instrument, making certain things?" "What have people paid you to do in the past or asked you to do for them?" As with the discussion of interests, the counselor may need to facilitate this discussion by introducing a few examples of his or her own abilities.

Following each general discussion, the group members should be given a few minutes to jot down their own interests and abilities. Ideally, each person will list at least 10 interests and 10 abilities. Clients should be encouraged to capture their thoughts in print or braille, unless they are unable to write; in this case, they should tape record their thoughts for future reference (a tone-indexed tape recorder is preferable to a conventional tape recorder because it allows for easier retrieval of information).

The counselor should have available for instructional-level clients some of the commercial interest and aptitude tests mentioned in Chapter 5. For nonreaders, the *Reading-Free Interest Inventory* (Becker, 1981) and the *Non-Reading Aptitude Test Battery* (U.S. Department of Labor, 1971) may prove helpful. For a general intelligence test, either the *Peabody Individual Achievement Test–Revised* (Markwardt, 1989) or the *Tests of Adult Basic Education* (CTB/McGraw-Hill, 1995) can be easily administered and provide adequate information for matching individuals to vocational settings.

Values are more difficult to discuss interactively due to the personal nature of the content. Therefore, a facilitator-led discussion of values—what they are, what words commonly describe people's values, and how one knows what people's values are without their telling—would be appropriate. (The counselor can use the values word list, Figure 5.2 in Chapter 5, for this activity.) Group completion of a values clarification exercise, such as the "Who Should Survive the Atomic Blast?" activity described in Chapter 5, can be helpful to clients who are unsure about their values. Depending on the congeniality of the group, the exercise can be assigned as an individual or a group effort. Sometimes, it can be entertaining to assign group members to represent the characters in the bomb shelter or to have open debates between groups of clients who feel strongly about certain characters. As cautioned in Chapter 5, however, because values clarification exercises may elicit strong reactions from group members, the counselor should not initiate activities he or she feels uncomfortable facilitating. Following group discussion, the counselor should ask clients to rank order their values. When presenting this task to the group, it is important for the counselor to discuss that individuals are likely to have to make value-related compromises throughout their lives and careers and that it is easier to live with compromises at the lower end than at the top end of one's rank-ordered value scale.

The final task in the self-awareness area is to capture information about liabilities. This is not an area for group discussion, but rather individual counseling. The counselor should encourage clients to limit their lists of problems or liabilities to the two or three things that are most bothersome to them currently. For a group activity, the counselor may want to facilitate a discussion of problem solving using the model explained in Chapter 8.

The problem-solving model includes the following steps:

1. Recognize a feeling of discomfort or pain (a problem)

2. Identify the problem through self-exploration

3. Understand the problem (how the person with the problem contributes, how others contribute, how the environment contributes, and what has kept the person from solving the problem)

4. Brainstorm possible solutions

5. Develop an action plan

6. Implement the action plan

7. Evaluate the results of actions undertaken

As for the informational-level clients, counselors will want to recommend that instructional-level clients read career planning books, such as Bolles's (1997) *What Color Is Your Parachute?* However, it may be more realistic for the counselors to read Bolles's material and incorporate it into their group and individual instructional activities with clients. Along this same line of thought, readers are encouraged to review the listing of career-related materials in the learning activities section of Chapter 5 for additional reading materials pertinent to the self-awareness content area.

Vocational Exploration

Instructional-level clients will need direction to use the career reference materials discussed in Chapters 6 and 10. Examples of completed job analyses, on which highlighted information that was retrieved from various resources can be very helpful in explaining to clients how to capture information from the references for themselves. An example is provided in Figure 11.1.

Another strategy for sharing information about job analyses with instructional-level clients is for the counselor and/or client to solicit any job descriptions that may have been developed by the local office of the state employment (sometimes called workforce, industrial relations, or labor) agency or the state occupational information coordinating committee (for contact information, see the listing for the National Occupational Information Coordinating Committee in the Helpful Phone Numbers list on p. 126). Often, these agencies develop job descriptions or job analyses from the generic reference materials (*Dictionary of Occupational Titles, Guide for Occupational Exploration, Occupational Outlook Handbook*), but in a simplified format. Using simplified job descriptions as a springboard for discussion can make the reference materials far more meaningful and less intimidating. Then, the counselor can model for the clients how to go through the materials effectively: how to use the index, how to use the numeric codes to capture information from different resources, how to pull out the important information from the less critical information, and how to record the information in a retrievable format.

As with informational-level clients, the counselor needs to discuss the concept of informational interviewing and be sure that clients understand the critical points outlined in Chapter 10. Instructional-level clients may well benefit from practicing informational interviewing sessions with the counselor. If clients are having difficulty with

---

Job Analysis Form

Name: <u>Samantha Smith</u>   Date: <u>5/21/98</u>

Job Title: <u>Motel Desk Clerk</u>

Numeric Code (from *Dictionary of Occupational Titles* or *Guide for Occupational Exploration*): <u>DOT 238.362-010</u>

Purpose (reason job exists): <u>The desk clerk is the first point-of-contact for guests arriving at the motel.</u>
<u>The clerk helps guests check in or directs them to where they need to go.</u>

Setting (location and environment): <u>Clerks work indoors and behind the registration desk. They are</u>
<u>often standing for long periods of time. They use computers to check guests in or out of the motel. They often</u>
<u>work evenings, weekends, and holidays.</u>

Major Tasks (job duties): <u>Clerks help motel guests with: registration, room assignment, room keys, and</u>
<u>answering questions about services, check-out times, the local community, and so forth. They keep records of</u>
<u>who is in the rooms to advise housekeepers, telephone operators, and maintenance staff. They usually present</u>
<u>final billing statements and collect payment from guests (cash and credit card) and must be familiar with dif-</u>
<u>ferent rates. In some smaller motels, the desk clerk may also do bookkeeping, operate the switchboard, make</u>
<u>advance reservations, and provide cashier services.</u>

Qualifications (experience, education, special skills, licensure, etc.): <u>Most desk clerks have at a</u>
<u>minimum a high school diploma or equivalency, but many have some college. On-the-job training is required. Bilingual</u>
<u>skills are required in some communities and preferred in larger metropolitan areas that cater to foreign visitors.</u>

Additional Information: _____
<u>The Educational Institute of the American Hotel and Motel Association</u>

<u>P.O. Box 1240</u>

<u>East Lansing, MI 48826</u>

Figure 11.1. Job Analysis Form.

this activity, the counselor may want to demonstrate the art of informational interviewing for individuals or in front of a group of job seekers.

Job Maintenance

Instructional-level clients learn best about job maintenance when they can relate job keeping content to their lives. Therefore, a session in which the counselor has the group members generate a list of the attributes they would look for in employees they would hire and then compare those traits to themselves can be very constructive. This activity demonstrates to clients that their desired worker qualities are the same attributes they need to demonstrate to employers. This is the "perfect worker" exercise first described in

List employers in your community who hire people to do the job in which you're interested:

Company: Harvey Hotel

Address: 450 Main Street

Contact Person: Connie Evers

Phone Number: 596-2345

Company: Lazy Days Motel

Address: 600 Congress Avenue

Contact Person: Dale Paxton

Phone Number: 444-2550

Company: Holiday House West

Address: 20299 West Lydia

Contact Person: Mario Tamez

Phone Number: 209-7899

Company: _____

Address: _____

Contact Person: _____

Phone Number: _____

Figure 11.1. Continued.

Chapter 8. It can also be helpful when doing this exercise to discuss how employers' expectations change over time.

Another meaningful strategy for teaching instructional-level clients about job maintenance is to have clients evaluate their own work behaviors and habits, as well as those of their peers. An example of a simple worker evaluation is included as Handout D.2. In a job readiness skills group, it is important to let clients evaluate each other anonymously to maximize honest feedback for group members (see detailed instructions in Chapter 8).

Job Search

Instructional-level clients can often benefit from both modeling by instructional staff and written examples of job search techniques. It is particularly helpful to provide clients with forms to capture critical information during their job searches, as in Handout E.4. Job seekers need to capture the following kinds of information:

- Where to go (name of company, address, and telephone number)

- Whom to contact (person's name and telephone extension, if known)

- When to go (date and time)

- Outcomes (Did the client pick up applications? Did the client meet anyone new that might be helpful later? Did the client get to speak with anyone in a hiring position? Did the client set up an interview appointment?)

- Other things that need doing (Does the client need to send in a résumé or list of references? Does the client need to make follow-up phone calls, and if so when? Does the client need to do further research or contact other people?)

Another important component of a successful job search is time management. Clients must understand that a successful job search demands time and that their time needs to be scheduled as closely as if they were expected at a job on a daily basis. A job search is hard work. It can easily take 8 to 10 hours a day, 5 to 7 days a week. During a job search, clients need to maintain calendars so that they know where they are expected and when. It can be helpful to have clients share their schedules with one another and the counselor to reinforce this concept.

- -

What became of Juanita . . .

Juanita attended the Job Readiness Program faithfully. She was present and on time every day and worked diligently to complete her work. Don and the interns, Olga and Sandy, were enthusiastic and helpful. They helped her discover what she really wanted to do: work in a day-care facility. Then, they helped her fill out applications and practice her interviewing skills. Juanita carefully copied all the applications she could and kept them for future reference. She also decided to have her Personal Data Sheet laminated—it was the perfect tool to help her complete forms!

She enjoyed being with the Job Readiness Program participants. It was true that they all had a lot in common. They were all disabled, although in different ways, and they were all unemployed. However, it seemed they were all people who genuinely cared about each other and wanted to support each other. When the other group participants found out she was interested in childcare jobs, they started watching for openings and told her if they learned of something interesting.

Don and Olga helped her investigate a child development course at the local community college and encouraged her to enroll. When she landed her job at Totsville within 2 weeks of completing the course, they all went out to lunch to celebrate her success.

Learning Activities

▶ **Reading**

Review the content and forms in Azrin and Besalel's (1980) *Job Club Counselor's Manual* or Boerner's (1994b) *Job Seeking Skills Instructor's Manual* and (1994a) *Job Seeker's Workbook.*

▶ **Doing**

Develop a notebook of papers to share with instructional-level clients. Include the following: self-awareness exercise forms, vocational exploration information and an example of a completed job analysis, examples of completed applications for companies in the local vicinity, and examples of résumés. Be sure to include examples of applications completed both correctly and incorrectly for discussion purposes.

CHAPTER 12

Advocacy-Level Clients

Walter, known as Wally, is turning 18 this year. Although his mother is planning to celebrate his birthday with a party in the backyard, she knows the only attendees will be family members and the 12-year-old twins from next door. It seems so unfair! Why don't the kids from his school ever respond to the invitations she dutifully sends? They make polite excuses when she sees them in the afternoons when she picks up Wally. Was it a mistake to move him from the separate campus the district provided for students with severe/profound cognitive limitations? Is it too late for him to make friends? He is such a sweet boy, always smiling and doing whatever he is told to do. Granted he can be stubborn—like the day he didn't want to leave the baseball field, even though the game had long since ended! She could not make him understand that there would be no more baseball that day. She thought she was going to have to carry him out.

Worrying about the party led to worrying about after high school. If Wally is lonely now, what will it be like when he turns 22 and doesn't have school? The teachers keep talking about work, but who would hire Wally? What could he do? The encephalitis he contracted as a baby damaged his brain. He had never learned to read or write or even speak properly. She could understand some of his verbalizations, but she was his mother! She loved him and she would care for him until she died! Oh, God, she thought, please don't let me die before he does.

WORKING WITH ADVOCACY-LEVEL CLIENTS

Advocacy-level clients pose entirely different challenges to counselors and educators than do informational- or instructional-level clients. These clients are functioning well below average in most areas of academics and/or functional life skills. Advocacy-level clients require extensive intervention, frequently with one-on-one instruction or support, for life. Combinations of teaching methods are necessary to facilitate learning: verbal and/or signed instruction, demonstration, modeling, hand-over-hand instruction, pictorial and tactual cueing, and so forth. Interactive learning environments with coactive instruction is often most effective for advocacy-level clients. Information learned in one environment by advocacy-level clients will not typically generalize into new or different environments. Therefore, the learning curve for such clients is slower and more drawn out than for other clients.

These clients can benefit from a career counseling methodology; however, the counselor needs to work collaboratively with family members, job coaches, therapists, attendant care specialists, case managers, and others concerned about and invested in the life of the advocacy-level person. It is anticipated that such clients will require a steady level of support for life. They may need assistance with personal or home management, time or fiscal management, transportation, communication skills, vocational skills, job maintenance, or the like.

To best serve advocacy-level clients, counselors should either perform an ecological evaluation themselves or purchase an evaluation from a subcontractor to determine each client's current functioning level and occupational awareness. The ecological evaluation is one of the most legitimate ways to capture information about advocacy-level clients, because the evaluation occurs in the natural environment rather than in a clinical or academic environment. (A detailed explanation of the ecological evaluation approach is provided in Chapter 4.)

Self-Awareness

Although most advocacy-level clients cannot self-report data about themselves, some of this information can be gathered through observation and case folder review. However, counselors and evaluators must rely heavily upon significant others in the clients' lives to provide information about their interests, abilities, values, and liabilities. Of course, information gathered about clients (even from family members and significant others) must be verified through observation of clients in the environments where they are likely to produce the reported behaviors.

If the client can self-express, it is important to solicit information about interests, abilities, values, and liabilities directly. Suggested questions to pose include:

- What do you like to do for fun?
- What kinds of jobs are you good at doing?
- What kinds of things are important to you (family, friends, being alone, exercising, having money, having free time, etc.)?
- What kinds of problems do you have?

Vocational Exploration

In the vocational exploration area, counselors should make arrangements for multiple job trials in the community to determine where advocacy-level clients perform best and seem to be most satisfied. To achieve a good match, a compatibility analysis for a particular worker and job is critical. A compatibility analysis is similar to the discrepancy analysis that informational- and instructional-level clients perform. The counselor or job placement specialist writes out a personal profile for the client and compares that with the job profiles (or job analyses) he or she has compiled for each of the jobs being considered as placement options.

Job Seeking Skills

With assistance from a counselor, job coach, or trainer, many advocacy-level clients can actively participate in job seeking efforts. They will do best to have available to them a personal data sheet for completing applications or to have someone complete applications for them. A personal data sheet looks much like a résumé in format but contains the same kind of information that is required on an application. With a personal data sheet, an advocacy-level client's helper can copy pertinent information onto any application and there is no concern about misspelling or misinformation due to miscommunication.

With clients who have verbal skills, service providers should role-play interviews regardless of whether the client will perform the entire process. Because it is better to be prepared to the maximum extent possible, the counselor and client should role-play all alternatives they can conceive of that might occur. With nonverbal clients, the counselor should involve them in the interviewing process to the extent possible. For example, a deaf–blind client who cannot speak but is cognitively able should be involved in the same kind of interview role-playing in which a verbal client engages. If a nonverbal client can use an interpreter, the interpreter should be included as an appropriate support in the job seeking process.

If the client is unable to actively participate in the job seeking process, placement is the responsibility of the counselor, employment specialist, case manager, or significant other. To facilitate placement by others, a client portfolio can be extremely helpful. The portfolio should contain, at a minimum, a client's personal data sheet, references or testimonials from previous employers or trainers attesting to the client's work skills and behaviors, compatibility analyses (comparing the client's attributes to the kind of work being sought), and if possible still photos of the client at work or performing tasks similar to those required on the job. It can also be helpful to include examples of unusual (e.g., pictorial) instruction sheets, cue cards, and/or pictures of adaptive equipment the client will be using on the job. Finally, placement may require support from a job coach or vocational trainer, and an employer will need both verbal and written descriptions of what the support staff can be relied upon to do. The employer's responsibilities are addressed in the following section on job maintenance.

Job Maintenance

For advocacy-level clients to keep their jobs, it is important that they receive support, as necessary, from both coworkers and service providers. Coworkers and supervisory staff on the job site with clients are natural supports, who can sometimes provide the training and assistance that advocacy-level workers need. They are the typical supports for nondisabled workers. However, advocacy-level clients may also need support services that can be provided only by a job coach, a professionally trained employment specialist. In instances where an employer is too busy to provide extensive training or is unaware of the kind of assistance a person with severe disabilities may need to perform competitively, a job coach is an appropriate support.

Job coaches can facilitate the integration of individuals with advocacy-level needs by providing on-site vocational training, helping an employer with restructuring job duties, supervising work behaviors, introducing clients and coworkers to one another, and ensuring that the clients perform their jobs adequately and in a timely manner. Ideally, job coaches fade (or diminish their involvement) over time and increasingly rely on coworkers to provide the support necessary to train and supervise clients.

Behavior management programs may be necessary to maintain employment for some advocacy-level clients. With clients whose behaviors may occasionally pose a threat to themselves or others, safety is of paramount importance. Protection must be provided under such circumstances, and protective strategies may include removing the individual from the environment; removing tools, materials, or equipment; rearranging materials, equipment, furniture, or office accoutrements; and preventing the worker from making certain movements within the environment or physically restraining the worker (Powell et al., 1991).

Job Search

Supported employment and sheltered employment provide the majority of employment opportunities to advocacy-level individuals. Although supported employment is the preferred alternative in most cases, sheltered employment should not be ruled out as a vocational alternative. Client choice is the key for counselors trying to determine the best placement for their clients. If a client or a client's family is committed to the client's participating in competitive work settings, supported employment is the most appropriate placement alternative. However, if the client or client's family is not committed or interested in the client's participation in a competitive work setting, sheltered employment may well provide a vehicle for participation in the labor market. Many Lighthouses for the Blind and Workshops for People with Developmental Disabilities have expanded the range of opportunities available to clients. They may offer sheltered and supported employment opportunities, as well as vocational evaluation, training, and work adjustment services.

Supported employment is an alternative to unassisted involvement in competitive work environments. In this model, assistance is provided, as needed and for as long as needed, by a job coach or work trainer/supervisor. The rationale for supported employment is to provide training to workers with multiple disabilities in the environments where they will be expected to perform: at their work sites. Supported employment also guarantees employers that they will be provided with workers who can perform at competitive levels immediately upon hiring. If an individual with multiple disabilities cannot perform the entire sequence of a job or perform quickly enough to meet competitive standards initially, the job coach is expected to facilitate. The critical element for success in a supported employment situation is that the job is accomplished in a timely and satisfactory manner. The different kinds of supported employment models are described in detail in the following sections.

Individual Placement

In the individual placement model, clients are placed in competitive environments with nondisabled workers only. They may work temporarily with support staff, job coaches in particular, but the goal is to use natural supports (coworkers and on-site supervisors) as quickly and efficiently as possible. Natural supports are typically coworkers, without disabilities, who are already on the job and would normally provide support such as on-the-job training to any new staff person. However, it is often necessary to facilitate integration with a job coach who is aware of disability-specific needs and tools or techniques to compensate for a client's disabilities.

The advantages of the individual placement model are that it encourages full inclusion of people with disabilities into the workforce, it provides a reality-based learning experience that cannot be paralleled in a classroom or facility-based work environment, and it provides the maximum amount of natural supports and consequences for behavior. The disadvantages are that workers with disabilities may be segregated by their coworkers due to stereotypic notions of what they can and cannot do, workers with disabilities may not receive the amount or type of supports they need to perform best and most independently, and there may be little flexibility to allow for differences in stamina or ability to learn and generalize information related to the job.

Enclaves

In an enclave model, an individual is placed with other people with disabilities in a competitive work environment. For example, an individual might work in a factory with a group of fellow clients or coworkers with disabilities. They might have a section of the work space and be responsible for a piece of the action. Enclaves are essentially work teams, comprised entirely of individuals with disabilities, working with teams of nondisabled workers in private or public sector businesses. Ideally, all the workers (with and without disabilities) share common areas, such as the cafeteria or breakroom space, and mingle during nonwork time and for social purposes. Enclaves typically are supervised by an employee of a rehabilitation agency, an employee of a nonprofit facility, or public school instructional staff. However, the supervision and training of enclave staff are sometimes performed in concert with or by on-site nondisabled employees.

The advantages of an enclave model are that workers with disabilities are stationed in a standard business setting rather than a sheltered setting and are encouraged to mingle with their nondisabled coworkers. The disadvantages are that, as a general rule, there is still an element of segregation or isolation due to the nature of the placement and minimal opportunity for movement into the mainstream plant activity.

Mobile Work Crews

Mobile work crews are groups of people with (usually) similar disabilities who travel and work together doing contract labor. They might contract to do janitorial services, pick up trash beside the roadways, do lawn maintenance, or the like. They typically travel to and from work sites with a job coach, trainer, or supervisor, and work together at the work site as a team or crew. Often, the crew divides up the work they have contracted to do and each worker does the portion of the job that he or she does best.

The advantages of a mobile work crew are that workers can be responsible for a part of a job rather than the whole; they have close supervision and support from specially trained personnel; transportation is typically provided, which is important for individuals with mobility impairments; and there is usually opportunity for contact with nondisabled people both at the job site and/or with customers. The disadvantages are that workers may be somewhat isolated and outside of the traditional workforce, there may not be a great deal of transferability to mainstream work situations, and there is often a void of natural supports.

· ·

What became of Wally . . .

When Wally's special education teacher, Ms. Smith, suggested that Wally's family, friends, and service providers get together informally to discuss his future, Wally's mother, Pat, thought it was a good idea. Ms. Smith explained that this kind of a meeting was known as Personal Futures Planning (PFP). PFP is an organized approach to life planning that includes a group of people (called a circle of support) who know and care about the student with a disability. The group defines what it sees working for the student in both the present and the future. Their ideas and dreams are captured using highly descriptive graphics known as maps. There is no formal paperwork, like an Individualized Education Program or an Individualized Program Plan; however, group members (with the involvement of the student to the maximum extent possible) develop an action plan to guide the group's efforts.

Pat said she would like to have the PFP meeting at her house. Ms. Smith appreciated her offering to host the meeting and said she would bring cookies. They chose a date and time they thought would be convenient for most people. Then, together they sat down with Wally to draw up a list of people to invite.

Learning Activities

▶ **Reading**

Many books are available that discuss the needs of individuals with severe, multiple disabilities. Many of the individuals described in these books are cognitively impaired or have cognitive impairment in conjunction with other physical or sensory disabilities. Many of the people discussed in these books are considered advocacy-level clients. Everson's (1993) book, *Youth with Disabilities: Strategies for Interagency Transition Programs,* focuses on services to deaf–blind clients. Both *Getting Employed, Staying Employed: Job Development and Training for Persons with Severe Handicaps* by Mcloughlin, Garner, and Callahan (1987) and *Supported Employment: Providing Integrated Employment Opportunities for Persons with Disabilities* by Powell et al. (1991) focus on the needs of individuals with developmental disabilities.

▶ **Doing**

Spend some time (1 day to 1 week) shadowing an advocacy-level client. With permission, observe the client at home, work, school, and/or community activities (e.g., shopping, attending religious services, recreating). Keep a journal of your observations.

Future Issues
and Resources

CHAPTER 13

Future Trends

Sandra left the rehabilitation center with a twinge of nostalgia. She had just finished her internship and still had questions: Where would she be working in the coming months? Would she join a public agency's staff or go to work with a private concern? If she went private, would she go with a for-profit or a not-for-profit organization? What was likely to become of the rehabilitation and career counseling profession? To simply stay at the rehabilitation center would have suited Sandra just fine. Unfortunately, the rehabilitation center currently had no job openings. She had heard all kinds of rumors during her internship, ranging from comments about the demise of the rehabilitation system to concerns from some rehabilitation workers and enthusiasm from others about a client voucher system.

Sandra decided to discuss her concerns with her university supervisor, Dr. Watson. Dr. Watson suggested she do some research into current federal and state rehabilitation legislation. Before Sandra headed to the library, they developed a list of questions:

- What is the current status of rehabilitation services in the United States?

- How will amendments to the Rehabilitation Act affect services to people with disabilities and the individuals charged with providing needed services?

- Does the Rehabilitation Act specify what services are to be provided to people with disabilities?

- What are the criteria for providing rehabilitation services?

- What is the likelihood that eligibility criteria will be dropped and rehabilitation services will be mandated like special education services for all people with disabilities?

- What is the status of private rehabilitation services?

- Will there eventually be a voucher system allowing clients to choose from an array of public and private service providers what they want and from whom?

Sandra wanted to investigate rehabilitation services further to see if she could predict where the jobs might be in the future and whether she would be able to compete for them. If she wasn't able to secure employment in a rehabilitation agency, would she be comfortable in another environment? What choices were available to her?

FUTURE TRENDS IN CAREER COUNSELING FOR PEOPLE WITH DISABILITIES

In the Rehabilitation Act Amendments of 1992 (P.L. 102-569), certain philosophical factors were emphasized. Although employment outcomes were identified as priorities, an ongoing commitment to independent living services was clearly stated as well. In addition, there was a reemphasis on the importance of client involvement throughout the rehabilitation process. Although these were not new philosophies, they underscored the Rehabilitation Services Administration's commitment to client outcomes—employment and independent living—as well as to the absolute necessity to involve clients in their rehabilitation programs. The following sections detail the philosophical underpinnings of the rehabilitation movement and their impact on career counseling for people with disabilities.

Self-Advocacy/Self-Determination

Of all the previously stated factors, none has more significance than the reemphasis on client involvement in the *entire* rehabilitation process. Although there has always been a mandated alliance between counselors and clients in the rehabilitation process, individuals with disabilities often felt their role was circumscribed by the authority of the rehabilitation counselors. In large part, this was due to the fact that the counselor had the final decision-making authority in terms of how to spend rehabilitation monies.

With mandated client involvement, the rehabilitation counselor and client together determine what services will be necessary for the client to gain employment. Career counseling may be provided by the rehabilitation counselor or subcontracted through a community-based counselor. Counseling and guidance services through federally funded rehabilitation programs are provided at no expense to eligible rehabilitation clients. However, career counseling services provided under contract to a counselor outside of an agency are paid for by a rehabilitation agency only if a client meets the agency's income eligibility criteria and both the counselor and the client agree that such services would be beneficial. If a rehabilitation client chooses and is eligible for private career counseling, the service must be included on the client's Individualized Written Rehabilitation Program.

Some adults with disabilities choose not to work with state rehabilitation agencies. Community-based career counselors may prove helpful as these individuals negotiate the labor market and make career plans. However, very few mainstream counselors have worked with people with disabilities. Therefore, individuals with disabilities who need disability-specific information or resources would be well advised to seek out the services of a rehabilitation counselor. Rehabilitation counselors can be found in both state and private rehabilitation agencies. Occasionally, private counselors with rehabilitation credentials work outside of facilities or agencies; they can typically be found through the information pages in telephone directories or, in states that offer licensure, through the licensing authority's directory services. In such instances, the client assumes fiscal responsibility for the services provided.

Self-advocacy begins with individuals determining what services they need, from whom they need those services, where services will be provided, and when services will be delivered. Self-advocacy does not mean that clients always get what they want. It simply means that an individual makes his or her needs known and negotiates in an assertive manner with other concerned parties—counselor, family, friends, and significant others—to get what he or she needs. Most clients know what is best for themselves; they are adults and should have the prerogative of making choices they can live with and feel good about. As mentioned earlier in this book, only truly advocacy-level clients need others to make decisions for them. Advocacy-level clients are unable to self-advocate and, therefore, must have others advocate for them. Their advocates may be family members, significant others, court-appointed advocates, or private (for-profit or not-for-profit) case managers.

Family Involvement

For many people with disabilities, the family network is the greatest source of support. Involved family members may facilitate in career and life planning sessions with rehabilitation and education personnel. Family members often provide assistance with housing, transportation, and many other life supports. They can sometimes tap into their own networks to uncover job leads and help with referrals for work. Most important, they provide emotional support to the individual with a disability.

For many individuals with severe, multiple disabilities who are advocacy-level clients, family members frequently play a pivotal role in developing their life and career plans. A family member often serves as the client's advocate and case manager. This makes sense in many cases because the family member knows the client better than anyone else— knows what the individual likes and dislikes, what his or her talents and weaknesses are, what motivates the person and what does not, and how best to teach the client new skills or reinforce present abilities.

Counselors need to involve clients' family members whenever possible and feasible. Family members may want or need to be included in clients' career planning and implementation. Informational- and instructional-level clients need to determine whether they want their family members involved in career counseling. If clients plan to solicit aid from family members in their life career plans, it is imperative that the people from whom they want or need things attend the counseling and planning sessions dealing with those issues.

Case Management

Family members often serve as case managers for clients unable to coordinate their own rehabilitation services. However, sometimes a family member becomes confused or frustrated by the different eligibility rules and/or agency regulations governing service provision, or a family member is no longer available due to death or abandonment. Therefore, independent case management has become a popular alternative to family-driven case management. A third-party case manager can help families understand what types of services are available and which might be beneficial to a family member with a disability. Private case managers may be hired by nonprofit agencies to facilitate in situations where an individual with a disability is unable to advocate for himself or herself.

Numerous guides to rehabilitation case management have been written for practitioners, but contain information that is useful to anyone with case management responsibilities. *Rehabilitation Caseload Management: Concepts and Practice* (Cassell & Mulkey, 1985) and *Case Management and Rehabilitation Counseling: Procedures and Techniques* (Roessler & Rubin, 1992) are particularly informative. The authors make clear to readers the case management demands of traditional rehabilitation counselors. For prospective rehabilitation counselors, they are "must read" books.

The future of career counseling for people with disabilities rests with clients, often referred to as consumers or customers by public sector rehabilitation professionals. The choices that people with disabilities make about where to go for services and from whom they would like to receive services will continue to exert influence on the Rehabilitation Services Administration. The current Rehabilitation Act, as amended, will expire at the end of 1997. Despite legislative threats in 1995 to consolidate rehabilitation services with other federally funded workforce development and job training programs, advocates for specialized services to people with disabilities convinced Congress that "one-stop shopping" (blending job training and placement services for people with and without disabilities) would be harmful to rehabilitation clients. This issue undoubtedly will be revisited in 1997, and rehabilitation service providers will be encouraged to work cooperatively with other agencies providing vocational services to the general population. People with disabilities will continue to see their roles strengthened and expanded in the rehabilitation process. Overall, the Rehabilitation Act continues to parallel the progress being made by people with disabilities toward full integration in the United States (Stafford, 1995).

Private Rehabilitation Services

In addition to the career counseling services available through the federal vocational rehabilitation system, many private rehabilitation practitioners provide career counseling and case management services to people with disabilities. Large numbers of private rehabilitation counselors are employed by insurance companies to facilitate in return-to-work programs for their recipients who sustain disabling injuries. The medical community has also expanded its efforts to provide holistic care with rehabilitation facilities, particularly for individuals with age-related disabilities, such as strokes, and survivors of head injuries who often require extensive medical intervention as well as rehabilitation therapies and career counseling. Many of these private medical facilities hire rehabilitation counselors to coordinate transition from hospital to community services and provide career planning and placement for patients. In addition, many new rehabilitation counselors are finding employment opportunities in the private, nonprofit sector. Consumer organizations working with people with specific disabilities, such as blindness, cerebral palsy, deafness, mental retardation, and so forth, also hire rehabilitation counselors to perform case management functions.

Technological Advances

In some ways, technology has been the great equalizer for people with disabilities. Computers with speech or braille output for people with severe visual impairments and voice-activated computers for people with severe motor impairments have dramatically improved their lives in many ways. Televisions with built-in captioning for deaf people and the capacity for audio description for blind people have improved their ability to access information. Motorized wheelchairs and new lighter weight metal alloys, in addition to hydraulic lifts into adapted motor vehicles, have diminished the mobility difficulties encountered by many paraplegics and quadriplegics in years past. With the passage of the Americans with Disabilities Act of 1990, many physical barriers have been removed or modified with technology such as electronic door openers.

However, technology has not been a panacea for all people with disabilities. Graphical User Interfaces (GUIs), with their reliance on icons to help people make programmatic selections, have been difficult to access by people with visual impairments. Likewise, the rash of touch screen controls make some appliances from rangetops to VCRs inaccessible to people with visual impairments. When cellular phones were first introduced, they were incompatible with many hearing aids and caused great duress to hearing aid users. Until these issues are resolved, technology will be a barrier to employment and quality of life for some people with disabilities.

Special Issues

Many issues facing the larger society are also issues for people with disabilities: multiculturalism, women's issues, the aging society, diminishing resources, an ever-increasing transient population, the AIDS epidemic, and overpopulation. The following are some facts about some of these issues:

- There are greater proportions of people with disabilities among minority groups than in the majority population of the United States (Asbury, Walker, Maholmes, Rackley, & White, 1991; Bowe, 1983; Kraus & Stoddard, 1989; McNeil, 1993).

- Women, particularly older women, report being limited in activity (by disabling conditions) more than men (Kraus & Stoddard, 1989; McNeil, 1993).

- Over half of the elderly population is functionally limited (in seeing, hearing, reaching, walking, or performing mental tasks) and about 4 out of 10 are limited in activity (Kraus & Stoddard, 1989; McNeil, 1993).

- Estimates are that in 1996 approximately 548,100 people were living with AIDS (many of them with disabilities caused by the virus) in the United States (Center for Disease Control, 1996).

- Close to 1 million people were estimated to be HIV seropositive (Rosenberg, 1995).

Many of these factors will have increasing consequences into the 21st century. More people with greater needs will reach out for services from rehabilitation professionals. Rehabilitation professionals will need to stay abreast of the changing population and a rapidly changing marketplace. Use of technology and the demand to be computer literate will increase for both counselors and clients. Creative approaches to service delivery must be explored: outreach efforts into communities rather than center-based services, group training opportunities in community schools and colleges rather than traditional university-based postsecondary training, and so forth.

Learning Activities

▶ Reading

Read Spraycar's (1995) book, *Stedman's Medical Dictionary* (26th ed.), or Bleck and Nagel's (1982) book, *Physically Handicapped Children: A Medical Atlas for Teachers.* Go to the library and peruse the rehabilitation and special education journals. Review three or four articles dealing with current themes of interest to you.

▶ Doing

Collect as many catalogs of adapted aids and appliances for people with disabilities as you can find. Contact local rehabilitation agencies, hospitals, and nursing homes to ask from whom they buy adaptive equipment. Ask people you know with disabilities from whom they purchase assistive devices. Look in the telephone book Yellow Pages for listings under medical suppliers, assistive devices, adapted equipment, and so forth.

CHAPTER 14

National, State, and Local Resources

Martin would start his new job in 2 weeks and he thought he should prepare by gathering some of the resource materials he had seen and used during his internship. He was convinced that the success of his mentor, Paul Adkins, was based in large part on his ability to find the kind of information his clients needed. Martin decided to call Paul and request a visit with him about what information to collect first. Although Martin would be in a far more rural community than Paul, he felt confident that Paul would have some good ideas. He called and left a message asking Paul if he could visit him. Then, he sat down to make a list of questions to pose to Paul. Later Paul called and set a time for a meeting with Martin.

When Martin arrived as scheduled, he and Paul spent a few minutes getting caught up. They hadn't seen each other in a couple of months and Paul wanted to know all the details about Martin's new job. Martin told him about the job and explained his mission for this meeting—he admired Paul's ability to access pertinent information for his clients and thought he would try to emulate Paul's approach in his new job, but he was feeling a bit overwhelmed and hoped Paul might give him some guidance. Paul suggested that Martin write down the typical kinds of questions he anticipated from his clients and then they could generate listings of materials, people, or organizations that might be helpful.

At the top of the list were questions about employment opportunities and supports, agency-provided employment assistance, and general questions about employers' expectations and responsibilities under the Americans with Disabilities Act (ADA). The other categories they listed (based on Paul's clients' typical questions) were transportation options, vocational and academic training alternatives, community resources, personal and independent living supports, recreation and leisure opportunities, consumer organizations, legislative information, Social Security benefits, medical and mental health–related concerns, and adapted technology, including aids and appliances. Paul also suggested including professional organizations on his list for Martin's own growth and to provide him with opportunities for input from colleagues.

• •

. . . Here's what he ended up with!

CAREER COUNSELING RESOURCES

National Resources

Employment

The federal government through the Department of Labor (DOL) produces many varied publications in the employment area. *The Occupational Outlook Quarterly* and *The Monthly Labor Review* are journals that provide current information about the general labor market. Both journals can be used in conjunction with the generic DOL resources discussed previously in this book, the *Dictionary of Occupational Titles*, *Guide for Occupational Exploration*, and *Occupational Outlook Handbook*, or used as stand-alone reference materials.

In addition, the DOL produced the Secretary's Commission on Achieving Necessary Skills (SCANS) materials, a series of publications designed to help educators better understand what competencies employers are looking for in new workers. The series includes *What Work Requires of Schools* (SCANS, 1991b), the initial SCANS report which is available in English and Spanish; *Skills and Tasks for Jobs* (SCANS, 1992b), a comprehensive guide for high school curricula development using the SCANS competencies with illustrative tasks; SCANS *Blueprint for Action: Building Community Coalitions* (SCANS, 1991a), which details how to develop a plan of action for educators, parents, students, and employers to prepare young people for work; *Learning a Living* (SCANS, 1992a), which includes detailed information about the SCANS process and gives examples of how the SCANS model has been integrated into schools throughout the United States; and *Teaching the SCANS Competencies* (1993), which provides expanded definitions of the SCANS competencies and describes how to infuse them into the school curriculum (also available in Spanish). Although the SCANS project completed its work, the publications produced are still available through the U.S. Government Printing Office.

The DOL Bureau of Labor Statistics publishes a considerable amount of information detailing trends in the labor market. The bureau publishes demographic information describing the labor force, including characteristics of employees with disabilities. It also provides industry input–output data and wage and salary information by industry. In addition, the Department of Commerce publishes U.S. Bureau of the Census population reports detailing the economic status of employed and unemployed Americans, including Americans with disabilities.

The following federal agencies are responsible for implementing the ADA employment regulations: Equal Employment Opportunity Commission (EEOC) and Department of Justice (DOJ). The President's Committee on Employment of People with Disabilities provides technical assistance materials and information on job accommodation (opportunities and supports, agency-provided employment assistance, and general questions about employers' expectations and responsibilities under ADA), tax incentives, and other employment-related topics. For individuals with mobility impairments, access to transportation is crucial to their employability. The federal agency responsible for implementing ADA transportation provisions is the Department of Transportation and Architectural and Transportation Barriers Compliance Board (ATBCB).

In addition to the public sector information available on employment, a number of commercially available products focus on national employment opportunities. Many of the current materials can be found in bookstores and public libraries. *Money*, *Business Week*, and other popular magazines publish listings of the top careers and employers for the year. In addition, there are popular, commercially available publications of specific interest to career counselors, such as *The Wall Street Journal's National Business Employment Weekly* (*National Business Employment Weekly* is available by calling 800/JOB-HUNT [562-4868] for subscription information or to locate a distributor). Popular books are published that list employers hiring in specific cities and states, nationally, and internationally. In addition, books are available that focus on job seeking in specific fields, such as law or environmental jobs, and areas such as federal jobs or temporary employment.

Vocational and Academic Training Alternatives

The Association on Higher Education and Disability (AHEAD) and the National Clearinghouse on Postsecondary Education for Individuals with Disabilities, also known as the Higher Education and Adult Training for People with Disabilities Resource Center (HEATH), both focus on programs providing postsecondary training to individuals with disabilities. AHEAD is geared specifically to personnel working with disabled students in postsecondary educational facilities, whereas HEATH provides information to both people with disabilities and service providers. HEATH provides information about programs, publications, and service providers with postsecondary education and training expertise, and publishes a resource directory biennially that lists national organizations with information on educational opportunities after high school for individuals with disabilities and an informative newsletter three times a year. All HEATH publications are free and available in print or on cassette (from the National Library Service for the Blind and Physically Handicapped or by request from HEATH).

Independent Living (Community) Resources

The American Network of Community Options and Resources is a national clearinghouse with information on community housing options for people with developmental disabilities. The International Association of Psychosocial Rehabilitation Services provides information related to psychiatric rehabilitation services. Finally, Life Services for the Handicapped is a national, nonprofit organization that serves individuals with all disabilities, except those with severe mental illness. Life Services hires private case managers who provide services to individuals with disabilities whose families cannot assist them and who are unable to manage independently.

Both the National Council on Independent Living and the Independent Living Research Utilization Program can provide individuals with information about accessible housing and personal care resources. Likewise, the American Disabled for Attendant Programs Today (ADAPT) provides information about such services as attendant care, financial management, transportation, and the like, to help people with disabilities live independently. Another resource is Accent on Information, a computerized retrieval system with data on products and devices to facilitate independent living.

The federal agency responsible for administering and monitoring Social Security benefits is the Social Security Administration (SSA). The SSA administers both the Social Security Disability Insurance (SSDI) program and the Supplemental Security Income (SSI) program. SSDI is the national contributory program that pays benefits to an individual whose income stops or is reduced due to retirement, disability, or death of a worker. SSI, on the other hand, is a noncontributory program that provides monthly payments to indigent people who are elderly, blind, or disabled.

Recreation and Leisure Opportunities

A number of national organizations provide information on recreational and leisure opportunities for people with disabilities, including Adventures in Movement for the Handicapped; American Alliance for Health, Physical Education, Recreation and Dance; American Camping Association; Boy Scouts and Girl Scouts; National Handicapped Sports; National Therapeutic Recreation Society; North American Riding for the Handicapped Association; and Special Olympics International. The National Institute on Disability and Rehabilitation Research's (NIDRR's) (1994) *Directory of National Information Sources on Disabilities* lists numerous sports organizations for people with different disabilities, ranging from bowling and skiing groups for blind people to wheelchair swimming and weightlifting organizations. The NIDRR directory also lists hundreds of organizations whose members have different disabling conditions and offer support to others with like conditions.

Legislative Information

Individuals interested in finding out about national legislation are welcome to call the Capitol Switchboard at 202/224-3121. For those with access to the Internet, Justice for All, a consumer organized and managed group that follows legislation relevant to people with disabilities, has an electronic bulletin board (JFA@TNET.COM) that is updated as events unfold. In addition, sites on the World Wide Web have information concerning national legislation. Two of the most popular websites are THOMAS (http://www.thomas.loc.gov.home) and FedWorld (http://www.fedworld.gov). Individuals also may write to the president, the Senate, or the House of Representatives. To write to the president, address the letter to The Honorable (President's name), The White House, 1600 Pennsylvania Avenue NW, Washington, DC 20500; the salutation should be written "Dear President (last name)." To write to a senator, address the letter to The Honorable (Senator's full name), United States Senate, Washington, DC 20510; the salutation should be written "Dear Senator (last name)." To write to a representative, address the letter to The Honorable (Representative's full name), United States House of Representatives, Washington, DC 20515; the salutation should be written "Dear Representative (last name)."

Professional Organizations

There are a number of professional organizations for career counselors, rehabilitation counselors, and special educators, including the American Counseling Association (ACA), the National Rehabilitation Association (NRA), and the Council for Exceptional Children (CEC). The American Rehabilitation Counseling Association (ARCA) and the National Career Development Association (NCDA) are ACA divisions. The Division on Career Development and Transition is a CEC division. In addition, there are professional organizations that focus on disability-specific concerns, such as the Association for Education and Rehabilitation of the Blind and Visually Impaired (AER), The Association for the Severely Handicapped (TASH), the American Speech-Language-Hearing Association (ASHA), and the American Society for Deaf Children (ASDC), or specific aspects of the career counseling process, such as the Association for Persons in Supported Employment (APSE), the American Association of Pastoral Counselors (AAPC), and Higher Education and Adult Training for People with Disabilities (HEATH).

State and Local Resources

Employment

State employment agencies, sometimes called workforce commissions or vocational guidance services, provide a wealth of information about state labor market demands and often offer supportive counseling and job search facilitation to unemployed applicants. An important service connected to state agencies responsible for employment services is the State Occupational Information Coordinating Committee (SOICC). In addition, many communities also offer job search assistance through Private Industry Councils and their community-based subcontractors.

Local employment offices operate in cities throughout a state with support from state-level agencies. Other public organizations that generate information about local employment opportunities include Chambers of Commerce, Better Business Bureaus, Job Corps, and Manpower Services. In many communities, job information banks or services are available through public libraries, newspaper listings, neighborhood recreation centers, and community school programs. Private employment agencies, career and vocational counselors, and outplacement firms also have information about local job opportunities.

Transportation Options

Mainline bus and rail services (administered by Metropolitan Transit Authorities) and paratransit services are available in many urban communities to people with disabilities. In addition, people with disabilities will often use taxis; contract (paid) drivers, friends, and relatives to provide transportation for them; or participate in car pools. Individuals with disabilities also may be able to provide their own transportation to and from work or school by walking, biking, or driving (with or without adaptations). Some people need modified vehicles; they may require wheelchair lifts or steering wheel–mounted controls or blocks on the gas and brake pedals. Other people need to "modify" themselves in a sense; they may use bioptic aids (lens-mounted telescopes) or drive only with license restrictions (e.g., only during daylight or off interstate highways). In some instances, rehabilitation or educational agencies may provide transportation; however, such arrangements are typically short term only.

Vocational and Academic Training Alternatives

State Higher Education Coordinating Boards monitor the programming available to people interested in postsecondary training. The participation of people with disabilities in postsecondary training programs is protected by law. Postsecondary training may include university or college undergraduate and graduate degrees, certificate programs in community colleges or vocational trade schools, apprentice or on-the-job training programs, and mentoring. Many rehabilitation facilities also offer specific vocational skills training to people with disabilities. For example, a rehabilitation facility may offer an office skills class for people with physical or sensory limitations using specially adapted classroom materials, such as computers with speech and braille output or voice-activated computers.

Legislative Information

State governors' committees for people with disabilities and local mayors' committees play a significant role in keeping people informed as to what is going on in their states and cities of interest to people with disabilities. In addition, at the state level, individuals interested in legislative information can go directly to their senators and representatives, governors, lieutenant governors, or other state officials. At the local level, interested citizens can contact city offices directly for legislative information. Local public libraries can help in locating these individuals or offices of interest.

Independent Living (Community) Supports

For individuals with severe health impairments or limited physical ability to care for themselves, attendant care may be required. Attendant care services can be located through health and human services agencies or via listings at independent living centers. Mental health and mental retardation agencies often publish directories that list providers of both attendant care and respite care. The state developmental disabilities council also may have information about where people with disabilities can get assistance with independent living and community supports. Social Security benefits, including health care, are managed at the state and local levels by representatives of the Social Security Administration.

Many rehabilitation and education agencies maintain technology departments that welcome contact from consumers and counselors regarding adaptive technology, including independent living aids and appliances. Many companies offer commercially available products for people with impairments of all kinds. Finally, Closing the Gap, an international source for information about microcomputer-related technology, produces a bimonthly newsletter and hosts an annual conference.

Consumer and Professional Organizations

Many local Chambers of Commerce publish directories of local chapters of professional organizations. In addition, the national headquarters of any organization of interest will be able to help locate local or nearby chapters or affiliates. If the local organization is able to maintain an office, it likely is listed in the telephone book or with directory assistance.

Recreation and Leisure Opportunities

State and city parks and recreation departments typically have calendars of events planned throughout the year. Although events are open to all citizens in the community, information often is available about which venues offer accommodations for people with disabilities. By law, all members of the community are supposed to have access to community-based facilities, such as neighborhood recreation centers, bowling alleys, swimming pools, tennis courts, and so forth; local museums and zoos; movies and theaters; and clubs and restaurants. However, individuals with disabilities may want to check with facilities before going to ensure ease of access. For example, not all shows at a theater are necessarily interpreted for deaf people or audio described for blind people. If a person has a special need, it is important to confirm that the need can be met in advance of showing up.

Learning Activities

▶ Reading

Find and review either a general directory of information about disabling conditions, organizations of people with disabilities, or resources for people with disabilities at the national level. An example was provided in this chapter, the NIDRR (1994) *Directory of National Information Sources on Disabilities.* Or, find and review a similar type of directory specific to a geographical area or disability type. For example, the American Foundation for the Blind produces a directory of services for people with visual impairments. Many local communities have directories available of services in the city, county, or state. If you are unsure about where to locate directories in your area, call a reference librarian and solicit aid.

▶ Doing

Use the Helpful Phone Numbers list (following this chapter) and select 5 to 10 organizations of interest to you. Call and solicit information. Capture information in some systematic manner: index cards, notebooks, manila file folders, or other.

Helpful Phone Numbers

ABLEDATA
800/227-0216

Accent on Information
309/378-2961

Administration on
Developmental Disabilities
202/690-6590

Adventures in Movement
for the Handicapped
800/332-8210

American Alliance for
Health, Physical Education,
Recreation and Dance
703/476-3400

American Association for
Vocational Instructional
Materials
800/228-4689

American Association of
Pastoral Counselors
703/385-6967

American Association on
Mental Deficiency
800/424-3688

American Camping
Association
317/342-8456

American Council of the
Blind
800/424-8666

American Counseling
Association
800/347-6647

American Disabled for
Attendant Programs Today
(ADAPT)
303/733-9324

American Foundation for
the Blind
800/232-5463

American Network of
Community Options and
Resources
703/642-6614

American Rehabilitation
Counseling Association
703/823-9800

American Society for Deaf
Children
800/942-ASDC

American Speech-Language-
Hearing Association
800/638-8255

Arc (formerly The
Association for Retarded
Citizens)
817/261-6003

Association for Education
and Rehabilitation of the
Blind and VI
703/823-9690

Association for Persons in
Supported Employment
804/282-3655

Association on Higher
Education and Disability
(AHEAD)
614/488-4972

AT&T Accessible
Communication Product
Center
800/233-1222

Boy Scouts of America
214/580-2000

Captioned Films for the
Deaf
800/237-6213

Center for Special Education
Technology Information
800/345-8324

Closing the Gap
507/248-3294

Council for Exceptional
Children
800/845-6232

Epilepsy Foundation of
America
800/332-1000

ERIC Clearinghouse
on Adult, Career and
Vocational Education
800/848-4815

ERIC Clearinghouse on
Rural Education and Small
Schools
800/624-9120

Federal Student Financial
Aid Information
800/433-3243

The Foundation Center
800/424-9836

Girl Scouts of the U.S.A.
800/223-0624

Hadley School for the Blind
800/323-4238

Higher Education and Adult
Training for People with
Disabilities (HEATH)
800/544-3284

Independent Living
Research Utilization
Program
800/949-4232

International Association of
Psychosocial Rehabilitation
Services
410/703-7190

International Center for the
Disabled
212/679-0100

Job Accommodation
Network
800/526-7234

Job Opportunities for the
Blind
800/638-7518

Life Services for the
Handicapped
212/532-6740

National Association for
Hearing and Speech Action
800/638-8255

National Association of the
Deaf
301/587-1788

National Center for Youth
with Disabilities
612/626-2825

National Clearing House of
Rehabilitation Training
Materials
800/223-5219

National Council on
Disability
202/272-2004

National Council on
Independent Living
703/525-3406

National Crisis Center for
the Deaf
800/446-9876 (TDD)

National Cystic Fibrosis
Foundation
800/344-4823

National Down Syndrome
Congress
800/232-6372

National Easter Seal Society
800/221-6827

National Federation of the
Blind
410/659-9314

National Handicapped
Sports/Disabled Sports USA
301/217-0960

National Head Injury
Foundation
800/444-NHIF

National Health
Information Center
800/336-4797

National Hospice
Organization
800/658-8898

National Information
Center for Children and
Youth with Disabilities
800/695-0285

National Information
Center on Deafness
202/651-5051

National Institute on
Disability and Rehabilitation
Research
202/205-9151

National Library Service for
the Blind and Physically
Handicapped
800/424-8567

National Mental Health
Association
800/969-NMHA

National Multiple Sclerosis
Society
800/344-4867

National Occupational
Information Coordinating
Committee
202/653-7680

National Organization on
Disability
202/293-5960

National Rehabilitation
Association
703/836-0850

National Rehabilitation
Information Center
800/346-2742

National Spinal Cord Injury
Association
800/962-9629

National Spinal Cord Injury
Hotline (24 hours)
800/526-3456

National Therapeutic
Recreation Society
703/587-5548

North American Riding for
the Handicapped
Association
800/369-7433

Orton Dyslexia Society
800/222-3123

President's Committee on Employment of People with Disabilities
202/376-6200

Resource Center for the Handicapped
206/271-0587

Social Security Administration
800/772-1213

Special Olympics International
202/628-3630

Spina Bifida Hotline
800/621-3141

TASH (formerly, The Association for Persons with Severe Handicaps)
800/463-5685

United Cerebral Palsy
800/872-5827

U.S. Bureau of the Census
301/763-8300

U.S. Department of Education
202/401-3000

U.S. Department of Education Information Office
800/424-1616

U.S. Department of Education Office of Special Education
202/205-5465

U.S. Department of Justice
202/514-0301

U.S. Department of Labor
202/219-7674

U.S. Equal Employment Opportunity Commission
800/669-3362

U.S. Government Bookstore
202/512-1800

Vocational Rehabilitation Hotline
800/222-JOBS

World Institute on Disability
510/763-4100

Young Adult Institute
212/563-7474

Recommended Readings

Azrin, N. H., & Besalel, V. A. (1980). *Job Club counselor's manual: A behavioral approach to vocational counseling.* Austin, TX: PRO-ED.

Berkell, D. E., & Brown, J. M. (1989). *Transition from school to work for persons with disabilities.* New York: Longman.

Boerner, L. A. (1994). *Job seeker's workbook.* Menomonie, WI: University of Wisconsin–Stout.

Bolles, R. N. (1978). *The three boxes of life and how to get out of them.* Berkeley, CA: Ten Speed Press.

Bridges, W. (1994). *Jobshift.* Reading, MA: Addison-Wesley.

Chopra, D. (1994). *The seven spiritual laws of success.* San Rafael, CA: Amber-Allen.

Clark, G. M. (1990). *Career development and transition education for adolescents with disabilities.* Boston: Allyn & Bacon.

Covey, S. R. (1989). *The 7 habits of highly effective people.* New York: Simon & Schuster.

Covey, S. R. (1994). *First things first.* New York: Simon & Schuster.

Crites, J. O. (1981). *Career counseling: Models, methods, and materials.* New York: McGraw-Hill.

Crystal, J. C., & Bolles, R. N. (1974). *Where do I go from here with my life?* New York: Seabury Press.

Davis, K., & Newstrom, J. W. (1985). *Human behavior at work: Organizational behavior.* New York: McGraw-Hill.

Department of Labor and Industries. (1982). *Employment orientation workshop . . . A job seeking skills class for injured workers.* Menomonie, WI: Materials Development Center.

Eberts, M., & Gisler, M. (1990). *Careers for bookworms and other literary types.* Lincolnwood, IL: VGM Career Horizons.

Everson, J. M. (1993). *Youth with disabilities: Strategies for interagency transition programs.* Boston: Andover Medical.

Everson, J. M. (Ed.). (1995). *Transition services for youths who are deaf–blind: A "best practices" guide for educators.* New York: The Helen Keller National Center.

Farr, J. M. (1988). *Getting the job you really want.* Indianapolis, IN: JIST Works.

Farr, J. M. (1988). *Job finding fast.* Mission Hills, CA: Glencoe.

Farr, J. M. (1991). *The very quick job search: Get a good job in less time.* Indianapolis, IN: JIST.

Figler, H. (1988). *The complete job-search handbook.* New York: Harry Holt.

Gaylord-Ross, R. (1988). *Vocational education for persons with handicaps.* Mountain View, CA: Mayfield.

Germann, R., & Arnold, P. (1980). *Job and career building.* Berkeley, CA: Ten Speed Press.

Gysbers, N. C., & Moore, E. J. (1987). *Career counseling: Skills and techniques for practitioners.* Englewood Cliffs, NJ: Prentice-Hall.

Hobson, R., & Sullivan, T. A. (1990). *The social organization of work.* Belmont, CA: Wadsworth.

Irish, R. K. (1987). *Go hire yourself an employer.* New York: Doubleday.

Keirsey, D., & Bates, M. (1984). *Please understand me: Character and temperament types.* Del Mar, CA: Prometheus Nemesis Book Company.

Kiernan, W. E., & Stark, J. A. (1986). *Pathways to employment for adults with developmental disabilities.* Baltimore: Brookes.

Krannich, R. L. (1983). *Re-careering in turbulent times.* Manassas, VA: Impact Publications.

Lathrop, R. (1980). *Who's hiring who.* Berkeley, CA: Ten Speed Press.

Levitan, S. A., & Gallo, F. (1988). *A second chance: Training for jobs.* Kalamazoo, MI: W. E. Upjohn Institute for Employment Research.

Levitan, S. A., & Johnson, C. M. (1982). *Second thoughts on work.* Kalamazoo, MI: W. E. Upjohn Institute for Employment Research.

Levitan, S. A., & Taggart, R. (1977). *Jobs for the disabled.* Baltimore: Johns Hopkins University Press.

Louis Harris & Associates. (1986). *The ICD survey of disabled Americans: Bringing disabled Americans into the mainstream.* New York: International Center for the Disabled.

Louis Harris & Associates. (1987). *The ICD survey II: Employing disabled Americans.* New York: International Center for the Disabled.

Louis Harris & Associates. (1989). *The ICD survey III: A report card on special education.* New York: International Center for the Disabled.

Louis Harris & Associates. (1995). *The N.O.D./Harris survey on employment of people with disabilities.* New York: The National Organization on Disability.

Ludden, L. V. (1992). *Job savvy: How to be a success at work.* Indianapolis, IN: JIST.

Marks, E., & Lewis, A. (1983). *Job hunting for the disabled.* Woodbury, NY: Barron's Educational Series.

Maslow, A. H. (1971). *The further reaches of human nature.* New York: Viking Press.

Matkin, R. E. (1985). *Insurance rehabilitation: Service applications in disability compensation systems.* Austin, TX: PRO-ED.

Mcloughlin, C. S., Garner, J. B., & Callahan, M. (Eds.). (1987). *Getting employed, staying employed: Job development and training for persons with severe handicaps.* Baltimore: Brookes.

Mendenhall, K. (1993). *Making the most of the temporary employment market.* Cincinnati, OH: Betterway Books.

Michelozzi, B. N. (1980). *Coming alive from nine to five: The career search handbook.* Palo Alto, CA: Mayfield.

Miller, S. E. (1996). *Civilizing cyberspace.* New York: ACM Press.

Myers, I. B. (1980). *Gifts differing.* Palo Alto, CA: Consulting Psychologists Press.

National Occupational Information Coordinating Committee. (1986). *Using labor market information in career exploration and decision making.* Garrett Park, MD: Garrett Park Press.

National Occupational Information Coordinating Committee. (1991). *Improved career decision making in a changing world.* Garrett Park, MD: Garrett Park Press.

Neff, W. S. (1985). *Work and human behavior* (3rd ed.). New York: Aldine.

Parker, R. M., & Szymanski, E. M. (1992). *Rehabilitation counseling: Basics and beyond.* Austin, TX: PRO-ED.

Patton, J. R., Kauffman, J. M., Blackbourn, J. M., & Brown, G. B. (1991). *Exceptional children in focus* (5th ed.). New York: Macmillan.

Porot, D. (1996). *The PIE method for career success: A unique way to find your ideal job.* Indianapolis, IN: JIST Works.

Powell, T. H., Pancsofar, E. L., Steere, D. E., Butterworth, J., Itzkowitz, J. S., & Rainforth, B. (1991). *Supported employment: Providing integrated employment opportunities for persons with disabilities.* New York: Longman.

Power, P. W. (1991). *A guide to vocational assessment.* Austin, TX: PRO-ED.

Rabby, R., & Croft, D. (1989). *Take charge: A strategic guide for blind job seekers.* Boston: National Braille Press.

Rogers, E. J. (1982). *Getting hired: Everything you need to know about resumes, interviews, and job-hunting strategies.* Englewood Cliffs, NJ: Prentice-Hall.

Seligman, M. E. P. (1990). *Learned optimism.* New York: Alfred A. Knopf.

Senge, P. M. (1990). *The fifth discipline: The art and practice of the learning organization.* New York: Doubleday.

Shapiro, J. P. (1993). *No pity.* New York: Times Books.

Shephard, R. J. (1974). *Men at work: Applications of ergonomics to performance and design.* Springfield, IL: Charles C Thomas.

Simon, S. B. (1988). *Getting unstuck.* New York: Warner Books.

Sinetar, M. (1987). *Do what you love, the money will follow.* New York: Dell.

Stovall, J. (1996). *You don't have to be blind to see.* Nashville, TN: Thomas Nelson.

Tieger, P. D., & Barron-Tieger, B. (1992). *Do what you are: Discover the perfect career for you through the secrets of personality type.* Boston: Little, Brown.

Wallach, E. J., & Arnold, P. (1984). *The job search companion: The organizer for job seekers.* Harvard, MA: The Harvard Common Press.

Wegmann, R., & Chapman, R. (1990). *The right place at the right time: Finding a job in the 1990s.* Berkeley, CA: Ten Speed Press.

Wegmann, R., Chapman, R., & Johnson, M. (1985). *Looking for work in the new economy.* Salt Lake City, UT: Olympus.

Wehman, P., & McLaughlin, P. J. (1980). *Vocational curriculum for developmentally disabled persons.* Austin, TX: PRO-ED.

Wehman, P., Moon, M. S., Everson, J. M., Wood, W., & Barcus, J. M. (1988). *Transition from school to work.* Baltimore: Brookes.

Wilcox, B., & Bellamy, G. T. (1982). *Design of high school programs for severely handicapped students.* Baltimore: Brookes.

Zunker, V. G. (1990). *Career counseling applied concepts of life planning* (3rd ed.). Pacific Grove, CA: Brooks/Cole.

APPENDIX A

· ·

Self-Awareness Handouts

· ·

Handout A.1
"I Like To" Checklist

Name: _____ Date: _____

I like to:

- ☐ work where I can think my own thoughts
- ☐ work with details
- ☐ work with ideas
- ☐ work with people
- ☐ work with tools, equipment, and other things I can touch
- ☐ work alone
- ☐ work as part of a team
- ☐ express my ideas
- ☐ see the results of my work
- ☐ help others
- ☐ work hard
- ☐ keep very busy
- ☐ keep things in good order
- ☐ take on new tasks

- ☐ look for other things that need doing when my own work is done
- ☐ do a better job than others performing the same work
- ☐ learn new things
- ☐ fill requests fast and accurately
- ☐ stick to a job until it is well done
- ☐ maintain a good appearance
- ☐ be around animals
- ☐ be around plants
- ☐ listen to music
- ☐ perform
- ☐ be outdoors
- ☐ be indoors
- ☐ do other things (give examples)

Handout A.2
Job Skills

Name: _____   Date: _____

Circle on the following list the skills that you have:

Confronting	Group facilitating	Writing	Representing
Meeting the public	Administering	Representing others	Working with precision
Terminating	Working in groups and teams	Controlling	Assembling
Coaching	Predicting	Organizing	Symboling
Appraising	Locating	Imagining	Handling stressful and awkward situations
Persuading	Promoting	Sensitivity	
Counseling	Interpreting	Creating	Dealing with pressure
Referring	Questioning	Monitoring	
Recruiting	Dramatizing	Selling	Reading
Fund raising	Developing mathematical models	Motivating	Listening
Teaching		Protecting	Repeating
Encouraging	Dealing with unknowns	Planning	Constructing
Accepting	Abstracting/ conceptualizing	Exhibiting	Repairing
Updating		Expressing	Cooking, culinary skills
Collecting and compiling	Processing	Proposal writing	Treating
Finding	Editing	Trouble-shooting	Printing
Timing and arranging	Caring for	Budgeting	Cultivating, growing things
Handling detail work	Politicking	Auditing and appraising	Using instruments
Initiating	Interviewing	Prioritizing	Laboratory writing
Researching	Processing and organizing	Typing and clerical ability	Assembling
Arranging	Delegating	Mediating	Setting up
Relating to people	Speaking	Sketching	Entertaining
Moving with dexterity	Handling complaints	Rewriting	Displaying
Obtaining information	Supervising	Translating	Operating
Designing	Confronting	Integrating	Making layouts
Deciding	Evaluating	Negotiating	Outdoor working
Record keeping	Reviewing	Analyzing	Corresponding
Inventing	Checking, inspecting	Programming	Mapping
Classifying	Observing	Managing	Measuring
Estimating	Expressing feelings	Serving	Musical knowledge
	Explaining	Anticipating	Debating
		Calculating	

Handout A.3
Self-Assessment Summary Sheet

Name: _____ Date: _____

Aptitudes

My current best aptitudes (abilities) are _____

My weakest aptitudes are _____

The easiest things for me to learn are _____

Interests

My highest interest areas are _____

My lowest interest areas are _____

The vocational interest I want to pursue now is _____

Values

My highest values are toward _____

My lowest values are toward _____

My set of values suits me well for these jobs (types of jobs) _____

_____

_____

Attitudes

I basically feel _____ about myself. This should affect my work in the

following way(s): _____

I feel best about _____

I feel worst about _____

My feelings toward other people are _____

This should affect my work in the following way(s): _____

My feelings about having a job are _____

My feelings about supervisors are _____

Expectations

I tend to see (myself, other things) as being in control of what happens to me. The good

thing about this is _____

but the bad thing is _____

My current job goal seems realistic because _____

_____

Handout A.3. *Continued*

Appearance

I want a job where I dress _____

My appearance causes other people to see me as _____

_____

_____

To improve the way I look, I need to _____

_____

Health

The only health problem(s) I have is (are) _____

These will affect my work _____

_____

Before going to work I need to do _____

_____ about my health.

The things about my job that might negatively affect my health are _____

_____

Mobility

The way I plan to get to job interviews and to work Is _____

_____

My backup plan is _____

Getting someplace consistently and on time is _____

_____

When I get a job, I will need help in _____

_____

Interpersonal Skills

I have _____ friends and find that I make friends _____

The major problem I have getting along with other people on the job is _____

_____

On the job, I like to work_____
(e.g., alone or with others, with people like or different from me)

I do (not) like being responsible for other people because _____

_____

I like interacting with people best when _____

_____

(continues)

Handout A.3. *Continued*

Work History

The jobs I have performed most successfully in the past were _____

_____

The longest I've held a job is _____

On the job I have a reputation as _____

_____

Based on my experience, other jobs I could do are _____

_____

When an employer sees my work history, he/she will probably think _____

_____

Functional Skills

When working, the major problems I have away from the job are _____

_____

I could really use some help in _____

APPENDIX B

· ·

Vocational Selection
Handouts

· ·

Handout B.1
Job Analysis Form

Name: _____ Date: _____

Job Title: _____

Numeric Code (from *Dictionary of Occupational Titles* or *Guide for Occupational Exploration*): _____

Purpose (reason job exists): _____

_____

_____

Setting (location and environment): _____

_____

_____

Major Tasks (job duties): _____

_____

_____

_____

_____

_____

_____

_____

Qualifications (experience, education, special skills, licensure, etc.): _____

_____

_____

Additional Information: _____

_____

_____

_____

_____

_____

Handout B.1. *Continued*

List employers in your community who hire people to do the job in which you're interested:

Company: _____

Address: _____

_____

Contact Person: _____

Phone Number: _____

Company: _____

Address: _____

_____

Contact Person: _____

Phone Number: _____

Company: _____

Address: _____

_____

Contact Person: _____

Phone Number: _____

Company: _____

Address: _____

_____

Contact Person: _____

Phone Number: _____

Company: _____

Address: _____

_____

Contact Person: _____

Phone Number: _____

Company: _____

Address: _____

_____

Contact Person: _____

Phone Number: _____

Handout B.2
Discrepancy Analysis Form

Name: _____ Date: _____

It is easier to reach your goal if you know specifically what that goal is. The following work-sheets will help you analyze your job goal to learn whether the goal you have set for yourself is realistic and suitable to your qualifications and abilities by comparing the skills, education, training, and other requirements of the job(s) you selected as a potential job goal with the skills, education, training, interests, and work experiences that you have.

Job Requirements for (Name of Job Wanted): _____
_____
_____
_____

Training: _____
_____
_____

Schooling/Education: _____
_____
_____

Skills: _____
_____
_____

Work Experience: _____
_____
_____

Physical Demands/Requirements: _____
_____
_____

Working Conditions: _____
_____
_____

Other: _____
_____
_____

Handout B.2. *Continued*

Matching Personal Skills/Qualifications with Job Requirements

List your current skills and qualifications in the same manner as you did above for the requirements of the job wanted (job goal).

My training: _____

_____

_____

_____

My schooling/education: _____

_____

_____

_____

My skills: _____

_____

_____

_____

My work experiences (related to job wanted): _____

_____

_____

_____

My physical requirements: _____

_____

_____

_____

Working conditions of job: Any problems or modifications required in order to do the job? If so, list. _____

_____

_____

_____

Other: _____

_____

_____

_____

_____

_____

(*continues*)

Handout B.2. *Continued*

Comparing the Two Lists

What are your strongest points regarding your qualifications for this job? _____

_____

_____

_____

What specific areas are you weak in? _____

_____

_____

_____

What qualifications are required for the job that you do not have? _____

_____

_____

_____

Are there any other problems to be overcome in order to prepare for or to be qualified for this job? If so, list. _____

_____

_____

_____

What do you plan to do to obtain the needed qualifications that you don't currently have or to overcome any problems listed above? _____

_____

_____

_____

Goal Setting

After reviewing the above information, is the prospective job(s) a reasonable job goal for you?
☐ Yes   ☐ No

If not, you may wish to discuss this problem with your vocational rehabilitation counselor in addition to the class instructor.

If it is a reasonable job goal, what do you need to do in order to achieve the job you want?

_____

_____

_____

_____

_____

APPENDIX C

· ·

Job Seeking
Skills Handouts

· ·

Handout C.1
Sample Skills Brief

Client's Name
Address
Phone Number

Education

Bachelor of Science Degree, Elementary Education, Southwest Texas State University,
San Marcos, TX

Participant in continuing education workshops related to counseling children with disabilities

Experience

- Casework manager for private agency working with children
- Teacher's aide in special education classroom
- Secretary at a probation office for juvenile offenders
- Motivational speaker
- Broadcast technician, women's news correspondent, volunteer coordinator for a radio station
- Volunteer coordinator for a disability advocacy group

Skills

- Adept at operation of Apple and IBM compatible computers
- Proficient with WordPerfect, FoxPro, Quicken, ProComm software
- Familiar with most office equipment, including dictaphone, copiers, ten-key calculator
- Typing speed of 60–65 wpm
- Research and writing abilities (WordPerfect 5.1 user)
- Classroom management skills
- Training and evaluation competencies
- Public speaking abilities
- Organizational and problem-solving skills

References

- Barny Smith
  400 East Main Street
  Dallas, TX 75700
  (214) 555-2200

  Dr. Aaron Wallace
  P.O. Box 3456
  San Marcos, TX 76700
  (512) 555-5992

  Dr. M. Irving
  150 Southwest Boulevard
  Dallas, TX 75700
  (214) 555-3890

- Ms. Pat Rose
  8705 Gallagher Lane
  San Marcos, TX 76700
  (512) 555-2113

  Mrs. Herman Munn
  32 Elm Street
  Dallas, TX 75700
  (214) 555-6350

  Mr. Michael West
  890 Westwood Drive
  San Marcos, TX 76700
  (512) 555-9855

Handout C.2
Calling for an Interview

Some things to remember *before* you call:

1. Have the correct phone number.

2. Have your personal data sheet with you.

3. Have a pen and paper with you to write down information.

4. Speak clearly and enunciate properly.

5. Use a phone where there are no distractions.

6. Be courteous and polite.

7. Do not have anything in your mouth.

8. When you are finished with your call, hang the receiver up gently.

Making the call:

1. My name is:

2. I am calling about your ad in the paper for a (state job of interest).

3. Is the position still available?

4. Are you interviewing for that position?

5. When may I come in?

6. What is the address?

7. Whom should I ask to see?

8. Thank you. I will see you at (time) on (day).

Handout C.3
Brief Personal Description

Many times a job interviewer will ask you to give a general description of yourself, frequently in the form of the statement, "Tell me a little about yourself." In asking this question, the interviewer wants you to share your skills and qualifications for the job as well as your personal qualities and outside interests in a succinct manner (2–3 minutes). You should use this opportunity to share the characteristics you feel make you the right person for the job. Some of the points to cover include:

1. An introduction
   Example: I am 34 years old and have lived in Texas all my life.
              I have lived in Austin since 1965.

2. Work skills
   Example: I am good with my hands and can use most power machinery involved in carpentry. I have 6 years of experience in house construction.

3. Short-term/Long-term goals
   Example: I'm looking for a steady job in carpentry that I can work at for a while. Eventually, I'd like to work into a foreman's job.

4. Work habits
   Example: I'm a hard worker, always on time, and good at solving problems. I have a reputation for doing excellent work.

5. Talents and interests
   Example: I have my own workshop at home and enjoy making wooden toys.

Your description may not include all of these points, but should include items 2, 3, and 4. Also, it is suggested that you make a list of several items for each of the points while preparing your brief personal description. This will provide you with the important items to share in your initial statement while giving you more items to share if the interviewer asks follow-up questions.

Even if interviewers do not specifically say, "Tell me a little about yourself," they may ask for the same information in other ways:

- Why do you want this job?

- What makes you a good worker?

- Give me an idea of your background.

- Describe your qualifications.

- Tell me a little about your experience.

- What's been going on with you?

There is no substitute for being prepared. Write a brief personal description and review it with the counselor or facilitator.

Handout C.4
Disability Statement

A disability statement is a to-the-point explanation designed to inform prospective employers of how you will perform on their job. It gives you the opportunity to discuss your disability positively in conjunction with your skills and qualifications. A disability statement is most commonly given verbally during a job interview, but you may also be required to share this type of information on an application.

Before preparing a disability statement, examine some of the reasons for doing so:

1. Your disability is or will become apparent to a prospective employer because it is indicated on the application (worker's compensation formation, reason for leaving past employment, gaps in work history).

2. Your disability is physically noticeable (limp, wheelchair, cane).

3. You may be recovering from an injury and still unable to perform some job duties right now, but will be able to later.

4. Your disability might become a problem after you have been on the job if you are asked to perform other duties prohibited by it (lifting, faster typing speed, a lot of time on your feet).

5. You require an accommodation or adaptive equipment to perform some tasks (magnifier, cane, wheelchair).

If these factors apply to you, then you probably need to write a disability statement. If they do not, then you may not need to write one. Discuss any concerns with the counselor.

If you conclude that you need to develop a disability statement, follow these steps:

1. First and foremost, develop a good interview format and style that emphasizes your skills and qualifications for performing the job. This is the most important and time-consuming step and the only way *anyone* gets hired.

2. Identify the potential problems with which prospective employers might be concerned. (For example, consider the following: Have you received Worker's Compensation, making you seem a safety risk? If you are still healing, how can you prove you will indeed become fully recovered? What will keep your disability from developing into a problem again? If you cannot see, how do you travel? If you cannot hear, how will you communicate with coworkers? If you cannot walk, how will you escape in an emergency situation?)

3. Custom design your disability statement, taking into account the prospective employer's needs and what you have to satisfy them. Therefore:

   • Prepare statements that recognize the potential problem.

   • Explain how it is no longer a problem and/or that you are able to use alternative methods to accomplish a task. For example, if you have received Worker's Compensation, perhaps you are fully recovered physically and received medical coverage in the settlement. In the case of a permanent lifting restriction, perhaps the job you desire does not require lifting and you can point this out. If you use adaptive equipment to travel, you may want to demonstrate how it works and describe your success in accomplishing related activities.

(continues)

Handout C.4. *Continued*

- Display a positive attitude by demonstrating your good communication techniques, being succinct (to-the-point) but thorough by addressing each point you identified and answering follow-up questions cheerfully. Think of yourself as "educating" the interviewer.

Timing in presenting your disability statement is very important. If your disability is not physically noticeable, it might be better to wait until after you have shared all of your qualifications before discussing it so as to keep the focus on your qualifications. If your disability is physically noticeable or if your application draws considerable attention to it, you may want to make a short opening remark that acknowledges your disability while indicating that you feel qualified for the job and that you will explain how. This allows you to put the interviewer at ease and still move into discussion of your qualifications. This method may require you to intersperse remarks concerning your disability statement as needed throughout the interview. No matter when you introduce your disability or how well you explain it, be prepared for follow-up questions.

Remember, everybody has competencies and deviancies whether or not they have a disability. The person able to competently share his or her qualifications in a succinct, positive, and relaxed manner is better able to eliminate or minimize the prospective employer's concerns and increase his or her chances of getting the job.

Write your disability statement and review it with the counselor or facilitator.

APPENDIX D

Job Maintenance
Skills Handouts

Handout D.1
Employer Expectations

Prospective employers have different expectations of you than others such as your friends. Employers are harder to please and their expectations reflect the primary company goal, which is to make a profit.

Furthermore, employer expectations change over time. Following are the employer's expectations of employees—and how they change over time—beginning with the job interview and continuing through the first day and week, first month, and first 6 months to 1 year.

The Interview

1. Be prepared
   - Get a good night's sleep
   - Eat breakfast
   - Bring a pen or pencil for notes
   - Bring your Social Security card
   - Have a driver's license
   - Have a neat and complete résumé

2. Act appropriately
   - Be on time
   - Be properly groomed
   - Be appropriately dressed for the type of work
   - Show a positive attitude:
     —Give a good handshake
     —Make eye contact
     —Pay attention and speak clearly
     —Have a neat application

3. Anticipate questions
   - Why you left other jobs
   - Why there are breaks in your work history
   - Why you want *this* job—you must know something about the company and position
   - Your education, training, and experience, and how they relate to *this* job
   - Clubs or organizations that show an interest in type of duties you may be performing, including hobbies
   - Special skills that are job-related (e.g., tools you can operate, being bilingual)
   - If you are a high school dropout, tell about GED or adult education efforts

4. Ask appropriate questions:
   - Think of what *you* want to know about the job (e.g., specific duties, details about hours, pay, hospitalization, vacation*, days off*, sick leave*, holidays*, etc.).

*Do not lead with these items.

Handout D.1. *Continued*

First Day and First Week

1. Be on time—work out the "bugs" before you are to first report to the job.

2. Arrange transportation—bus, car, etc.—and make a "dry run" 1 day early.

3. Dress appropriately—how to dress should be determined before reporting to work.

4. Make sure you are well groomed.

5. Make an effort to be cheerful and get along with everyone you meet.

6. Be willing to:
   - Be supervised closely at first
   - Learn and develop skills
   - Listen and pay attention to corrections
   - Ask questions if you don't understand
   - Establish your reputation as a worker by putting out good daily production (remember, it is difficult to change a poor initial impression)
   - Become more familiar with company policy

First Month

1. You must be on time because others depend on you. Take coffee breaks and lunch only when specified and only for the specified time.

2. Establish friendships:
   - Continue to get along with everyone.
   - Be aware of informal social structures like cliques and how you fit in.
   - Keep biased view of others to yourself.
   - Resist temptation to gossip and believe rumors.

3. Learn company policies:
   - Know written and unwritten policies.
   - Interact well with fellow workers and supervisor.

4. Be flexible in developing skills:
   - When in new areas, ask questions.
   - Show some increase in production and decrease in supervision needed.

5. Become accustomed to the new environment. You will have to adjust to your new surroundings, as in moving to a new house or apartment.

6. Be aware of your probation period:
   - It is a time of initial evaluation.
   - Learn the duties and responsibilities for yourself, supervisor, and others, and reevaluate your initial commitment.

(continues)

Handout D.1. *Continued*

6 Months to 1 Year

1. By this time, many things should be second nature, such as performing duties on time, using good time management, knowing company policies, and getting along.

2. Be willing to expand your skills through off-the-job training (GED classes, night school, company-sponsored courses) for early qualification for added responsibilities. This helps promotion potential.

3. Take the initiative:

   - Be self-directed; find work in slack times.
   - Anticipate requirements; don't need to be told.
   - Make appropriate suggestions based on increased experience, knowledge, skills, and so on.
   - These things help your reputation as a worker.

4. In the area of commitment to and by the company:

   - Think of your loyalty to the company and your identification with company goals.
   - Also, consider things like stock options, retirement programs, in-house training.

5. Finally, be cautious:

   - Don't develop a false sense of security in a good situation.
   - Don't take long weekends (i.e., sick leave on Monday and Friday).
   - Be careful if you take a second job not to let it interfere with your primary job.

Conclusion

Keeping these things in mind can help you keep and enjoy your job, and hopefully lead to promotion and advancement in your career field.

Handout D.2
Worker Evaluation Form

Name: _____ Date: _____

Evaluator: (optional) _____

	Good	Average	Needs Improvement
Attendance	☐	☐	☐
Punctuality	☐	☐	☐
Cooperation	☐	☐	☐
Appearance	☐	☐	☐
Friendliness	☐	☐	☐
Participation	☐	☐	☐
Follows instructions	☐	☐	☐
Asks questions when not understanding	☐	☐	☐
Doesn't allow personal problems to affect job performance	☐	☐	☐

Other comments: _____

_____

_____

_____

_____

_____

_____

_____

_____

_____

_____

_____

_____

_____

_____

_____

_____

_____

APPENDIX E

· ·

Job Search
Skills Handouts

· ·

Handout E.1
Action Plan Form

Name: _____ Date: _____

The top 3 kinds of jobs I am looking for are:

1. _____

2. _____

3. _____

I plan to look _____ days for number 1, _____ days for number 2, and _____ days for number 3.

I will look for job leads in the following ways: _____

_____

_____

Each day I will make _____ telephone calls.

Each week I will complete _____ applications.

The first place I am going to look is: _____

_____

I think the hardest thing for me will be: _____

_____

I feel that I could use some help with: _____

_____

I will need help from the following people: _____

_____

I will be disappointed if I don't:

• find a job in _____ days

• have at least _____ interviews in the next _____ week

Comments: _____

_____

_____

Handout E.2
Career Planning Sheet

The jobs I can do now are: _____

_____

_____

The jobs that I might like to do in 2 years are: _____

_____

_____

The jobs that I might like to do 10 years from now are: _____

_____

_____

To do the jobs I want 2 years from now, I will need to improve my abilities in: _____

_____

_____

_____

To do the jobs I want 10 years from now, I will need to improve my skills in: _____

_____

_____

_____

The biggest problem with the jobs I can do now is: _____

_____

_____

The problems I have with getting a job now are: _____

_____

_____

What can I do about it? _____

_____

_____

_____

Handout E.3
Career Plan

Name: _____   Date: _____

Long-Term Objective: _____   Projected Date: _____

Activity: _____

_____

Short-Term Objective: _____   Projected Date: _____

Activity: _____

_____

Short-Term Objective: _____   Projected Date: _____

Activity: _____

_____

Short-Term Objective: _____   Projected Date: _____

Activity: _____

_____

Short-Term Objective: _____   Projected Date: _____

Activity: _____

_____

Short-Term Objective: _____   Projected Date: _____

Activity: _____

_____

Short-Term Objective: _____   Projected Date: _____

Activity: _____

_____

Short-Term Objective: _____   Projected Date: _____

Activity: _____

_____

Short-Term Objective: _____   Projected Date: _____

Activity: _____

_____

Handout E.4
Contact Log

Name: _____ Job Title: _____

Job Interview: _____ Information Review: _____

Company: _____

Address: _____

Telephone Number: _____

Contact Person: _____

Date and Result of Contact: _____

_____

Date and Result of Contact: _____

_____

Date and Result of Contact: _____

_____

Company: _____

Address: _____

Telephone Number: _____

Contact Person: _____

Date and Result of Contact: _____

_____

Date and Result of Contact: _____

_____

Date and Result of Contact: _____

_____

Company: _____

Address: _____

Telephone Number: _____

Contact Person: _____

Date and Result of Contact: _____

_____

Date and Result of Contact: _____

_____

Date and Result of Contact: _____

_____

APPENDIX F

· ·

Blackline
Masters

· ·

Observation Checklist

Client: _____

Observation date: _____   Observation time: _____

Placement: _____

Observer: _____

Task(s) performed/skill utilization: _____

_____

_____

_____

_____

_____

Work Behaviors Observed	Yes	No	N/A
Is punctual	☐	☐	☐
Initiates work	☐	☐	☐
Follows instructions	☐	☐	☐
Attends to task	☐	☐	☐
Attends to detail	☐	☐	☐
Cooperates	☐	☐	☐
Works consistently	☐	☐	☐
Dresses appropriately	☐	☐	☐
Solicits help, as needed	☐	☐	☐
Problem-solves tasks	☐	☐	☐
Interacts with coworkers	☐	☐	☐
Follows work rules	☐	☐	☐
Attends to safety concerns	☐	☐	☐
Completes tasks	☐	☐	☐
Puts tools/materials away	☐	☐	☐

Comments: List overall strengths and weaknesses. Make recommendations. Note level of supervision required to perform tasks assigned. For example, can client perform tasks independently when given verbal, signed, or written instructions? Can client perform with demonstration or tactual cues? How often does the client require prompting to stay on task? Does the client respond to certain people in the work environment more favorably than others? Note accommodations necessary for the client to perform optimally.

Ecological Evaluation Process Checklist

Meet with the client to determine his or her vocational, social, academic, and independent living goals. It is important to spend time ascertaining the client's perception of his or her current performance and future needs in vocational, social, academic, and daily living skills areas. Inform the client of the nature of ecological evaluation and answer any questions. It is important that the client understand that, although you may observe him or her in activities without announcement, you will share with the client what you observed and the impressions you derived with him or her and/or his or her legal guardian/caregiver(s). (*Note:* This checklist can be combined with observation sheets by an evaluator.)

Review existing records (note date of reports and report writer)

Classroom teacher: _____
_____
_____

Specialists (orientation and mobility, occupational and physical therapy, speech–language therapy): _____
_____
_____

Psychological or neuropsychological: _____
_____
_____

Aptitude/achievement test results: _____
_____
_____

Medical reports: _____
_____
_____

Familial information: _____
_____
_____

Client's self-report: _____
_____
_____

(continues)

Ecological Evaluation Process Checklist. *Continued*

Observe (note location, others present, dates, and times)

Classes: _____

_____

_____

Cafeteria/restaurant: _____

_____

_____

Free time: _____

_____

_____

Dorm or home: _____

_____

_____

Therapy: _____

_____

_____

Work site: _____

_____

_____

Field trips/community activities: _____

_____

_____

Note dates, times, and locations of meetings with client and attach relevant outcomes (IWRP, IEP, ITP, IPP, other):

Meet with personnel providing services to client and note with whom you have met, how to recontact, date of contact, and any other relevant details:

Contact family members of client or significant others (attach copy of release of information) and note name, contact number and/or location, and date of contact:

Values Word List

Freedom	Recognition	Kindness
Creativity	Self-direction	Flexibility
Family life	Interdependence	Routines
Honesty	Caretaking	Education
Happiness	Cheerfulness	Serenity
Learning	Morality	Orderliness
Openness	Craftsmanship	Mobility
Aesthetics	Adventure	Friendship
Joy	Wisdom	Independence
Helpfulness	Wealth	Regard
Frugality	Solitude	Fame
Leadership	Religion	Affection
Athletics	Health	Privacy
Strength	Integrity	Fortune
Responsibility	Security	Nature
Beauty	Respect	Spirituality
Cleanliness	Generosity	Relationships

Job Analysis Form

Name: _____ Date: _____

Job Title: _____

Numeric Code (from *Dictionary of Occupational Titles* or *Guide for Occupational Exploration*): _____

Purpose (reason job exists): _____

_____

_____

_____

Setting (location and environment): _____

_____

_____

_____

Major Tasks (job duties): _____

_____

_____

_____

_____

_____

_____

_____

_____

Qualifications (experience, education, special skills, licensure, etc.): _____

_____

_____

_____

_____

_____

_____

_____

_____

_____

_____

_____

_____

_____

_____

Job Analysis Form. *Continued*

List employers in your community who hire people to do the job in which you're interested:

Company: _____

Address: _____

_____

Contact Person: _____

Phone Number: _____

Company: _____

Address: _____

_____

Contact Person: _____

Phone Number: _____

Company: _____

Address: _____

_____

Contact Person: _____

Phone Number: _____

Company: _____

Address: _____

_____

Contact Person: _____

Phone Number: _____

Company: _____

Address: _____

_____

Contact Person: _____

Phone Number: _____

Company: _____

Address: _____

_____

Contact Person: _____

Phone Number: _____

A Sales Approach to Job Seeking

Stage	Sales		Job Seeking	
	Activity	Activity	Result	
Pre-Approach	Product awareness and analysis	Client self-awareness	Awareness of employment strengths and weaknesses	
	Customer need awareness and analysis	Job market assessment	Awareness of job requirements and types of jobs available	
	Plan of contacts	Job seeking plan	List of places to consider	
Approach	Advertising	Telephone contact, letter of intent, application, résumé or vita	Appointments for interviews or other job leads	
	Product Presentation	Presenting worker qualifications, relate skills to job duties, answer questions	Get job or not	
	Answering objections	Acknowledge objections, supply information to counteract objections	Get job or not	
Closing	Making the sale	Get commitment for job, find out next step in process	Get job or make plans for follow-up	
Follow-up	Recontacting on a regular schedule	Call back to express interest or find out about other jobs	Keep active and keep employment doors open	

Personal Data Sheet

Name (First, Middle, Last)
Address (Street, City, State, Zip Code)
Phone (Include area code)
Social Security Number

Educational Experience:

School(s)
Location
Dates attended
Diplomas, degrees, or certificates received

Work History:

Company(ies)
Location
Supervisor
Dates of employment
Starting salary and ending salary
Job title and duties

Special Skills:

(Computer skills, software use—word processing, spreadsheets, databases; foreign languages
(verbal and written skills); writing skills (grants, reports, creative efforts); skills requiring licensure
(medical, physical or occupational or speech therapy, social work, teaching, counseling);
athletic performance or artistic efforts; compensatory skills, if appropriate for job; ability to
use hand tools and/or power tools; ability to drive or operate equipment; etc.)

Other Related Experience:

(Volunteer work, membership in school or extracurricular groups, etc.)

References: (This can be on a separate page, if necessary.)

Name, Address, Phone (work phone and fax, or home phone)
(Include three or four nonpersonal references)

Interview Critique

Name: _____ Date: _____

	Good	Average	Poor
Appearance	☐	☐	☐
Introduction	☐	☐	☐
Establishes friendly interaction with interviewer	☐	☐	☐
Brief personal description	☐	☐	☐
Explanation of disability	☐	☐	☐
Explains work experience as it relates to job	☐	☐	☐
Makes 3 positive statements about self	☐	☐	☐
Pays attention	☐	☐	☐
Ability to answer questions	☐	☐	☐
Ability to ask job-related questions	☐	☐	☐
Understands job duties	☐	☐	☐
Knows about company	☐	☐	☐
Body language	☐	☐	☐
Motivation	☐	☐	☐
Interest	☐	☐	☐
Seems competent/able to sell self	☐	☐	☐
Knows next step in hiring process	☐	☐	☐

Comments: _____

_____

_____

_____

_____

_____

_____

_____

_____

_____

The Onion Analogy or
Different Levels of Relationships

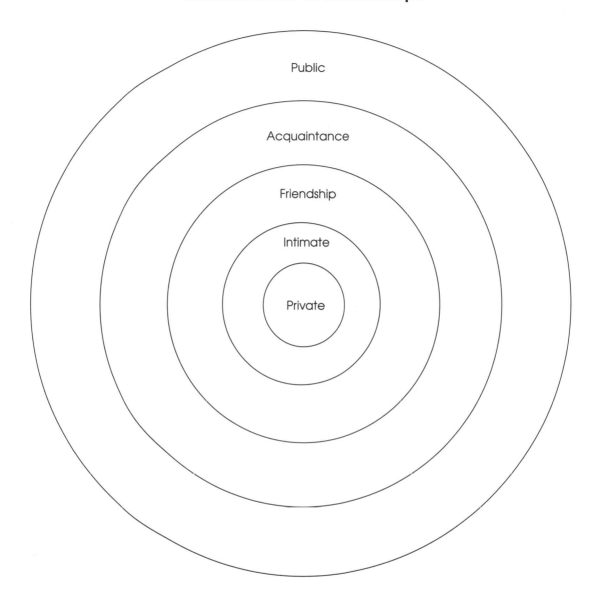

Public

Acquaintance

Friendship

Intimate

Private

Job Search Checklist

Name: _____ Date: _____

Organize job search time (daily activity)	☐
Identify appropriate job openings (minimum of 4 a day)	☐
Call to solicit job postings for openings identified	☐
Pick up (or have mailed) job applications	☐
Complete job applications	☐
Copy completed job applications	☐
Submit job applications	☐
Find out closing dates for jobs of interest	☐
Call to check application status	☐
Schedule job interviews	☐
Arrange transportation to interview	☐
Prepare for interview (clothes, supporting documentation)	☐
Interview for job	☐
Document job contacts (people, places, things)	☐
Send thank you note, if appropriate	☐
Follow up on job interviews	☐
Other _____	☐
_____	☐

References

Americans with Disabilities Act of 1990, 42 U.S.C. §12101 *et seq.*

Andrew, D. M., Paterson, D. G., & Longstaff, H. P. (1961). *Minnesota Clerical Test.* New York: Psychological Corporation.

Asbury, C. A., Walker, S., Maholmes, V., Rackley, R., & White, S. (1991). *Disability prevalence and demographic association among race/ethnic minority populations in the United States: Implications for the 21st century.* Washington, DC: Howard University.

Azrin, N. H., & Besalel, V. A. (1980). *Job Club counselor's manual: A behavioral approach to vocational counseling.* Austin, TX: PRO-ED.

Becker, R. L. (1981). *Revised Reading-Free Vocational Interest Inventory.* Columbus, OH: Elbern.

Bennett, G. K., Seashore, H. G., & Wesman, A. G. (1982). *Differential Aptitude Tests.* San Antonio: Psychological Corporation.

Bleck, E. E., & Nagel, D. A. (1982). *Physically handicapped children: A medical atlas for teachers.* Orlando, FL: Grune & Stratton.

Boerner, L. A. (1994a). *Job seeker's workbook.* Menomonie: University of Wisconsin–Stout.

Boerner, L. A. (1994b). *Job seeking skills instructor's manual.* Menomonie: University of Wisconsin–Stout.

Bolles, R. N. (1978). *The three boxes of life and how to get out of them.* Berkeley, CA: Ten Speed Press.

Bolles, R. N. (1984). What to do when you're feeling absolutely stuck in your job-hunt or career-change. *Newsletter About Life/Work Planning, 3,* 1–4.

Bolles, R. N. (1991). *Job-hunting tips for the so-called handicapped or people who have disabilities.* Berkeley, CA: Ten Speed Press.

Bolles, R. N. (1997). *What color is your parachute?* Berkeley, CA: Ten Speed Press.

Bolton, B., & Roessler, R. (1986). *Manual for the Work Personality Profile.* Fayetteville: Arkansas Research and Training Center in Vocational Rehabilitation.

Bowe, F. (1983). *Demography and disability: A chartbook for rehabilitation.* Fayetteville: Arkansas Rehabilitation Research and Training Center.

Brady, D. (1996, Fall). Federal news. *Together.* Austin, TX: The Arc of Texas.

Brolin, D. E. (1993). *Life centered career education: A competency based approach* (4th ed.). Reston, VA: Council for Exceptional Children.

Brown, D., & Brooks, L. (1991). *Career counseling techniques.* Boston: Allyn & Bacon.

Brown, D., & Brooks, L. (1996). *Career choice and development* (3rd ed.). San Francisco: Jossey-Bass.

Carkhuff, R. R. (1969). *Helping and human relations: A primer for lay and professional helpers* (Vols. 1–2). New York: Holt, Rinehart and Winston.

Carkhuff, R. R. (1993). *The art of helping VII.* Amherst, MA: Human Resource Development Press.

Carkhuff, R. R., & Berenson, B. G. (1977). *Beyond counseling and therapy.* New York: Holt, Rinehart and Winston.

Cassell, J. L., & Mulkey, S. W. (1985). *Rehabilitation caseload management: Concepts and practice.* Austin, TX: PRO-ED.

Center for Disease Control and Prevention. (1996, June). *HIV/AIDS surveillance report.* Atlanta, GA: Author.

Clark, G. M. (1990). *Career development and transition education for adolescents with disabilities.* Needham Heights, MA: Allyn & Bacon.

Corey, M. S., & Corey, G. (1992). *Groups process and practice* (4th ed.). Pacific Grove, CA: Brooks/Cole.

Covey, S. R. (1989). *The 7 habits of highly effective people: Powerful lessons in personal change.* New York: Simon & Schuster.

Crawford, J. E., & Crawford, D. M. (1975). *The Crawford Small Parts Dexterity Test.* New York: Psychological Corporation.

Crystal, J. C., & Bolles, R. N. (1974). *Where do I go from here with my life?* New York: Seabury Press.

CTB/McGraw-Hill. (1995). *Tests of Adult Basic Education.* Monterey, CA: Author.

Daniels, J. L. (1978). *Job Readiness Clinic final report*. Unpublished Department of Education Grant No. 44-P-81084.

DeVito, J. A. (1995). *The interpersonal communication book* (7th ed.). New York: Harper Collins.

Dial, J., Mezger, C., Gray, S., Massey, T., Chan, F., & Hull, J. (1992). *The Comprehensive Vocational Evaluation System*. Dallas, TX: McCarron-Dial Systems.

Education for All Handicapped Children Act of 1975, 20 U.S.C. § 1401–1420.

Everson, J. M. (1993). *Youth with disabilities: Strategies for interagency transition programs*. Boston: Andover Medical.

Fesko, S. L., & Temelini, D. J. (in press). What consumers and staff tell us about effective job search practices. In F. Menz, J. Eggers, & V. Brooke (Eds.), *Vocational rehabilitation research: Lessons for improving employment of people with disabilities*. Menomonie: Rehabilitation Research and Training Center at University of Wisconsin–Stout.

Friel, T., & Carkhuff, R. (1974). *The art of developing a career*. Amherst, MA: Human Services Development Press.

Ginzberg, E. (1972). Toward a theory of occupational choice: A restatement. *Vocational Guidance Quarterly, 20*(3), 169–176.

Ginzberg, E., Ginsburg, S., Axelrad, S., & Herma, J. (1951). *Occupational choice: An approach to a general theory*. New York: Columbia University Press.

Gottfredson, G. D., & Holland, J. L. (1989). *Dictionary of Holland occupational codes* (2nd ed.). Odessa, FL: Psychological Assessment Resources.

Hansen, C. E. (1975). *Job readiness clinic*. Unpublished Department of Education Grant No. 44-P-81084.

Hathaway, S., & McKinley, C. (1970). *Minnesota Multiphasic Personality Inventory*. Minneapolis: National Computer Systems.

Holland, J. L. (1985). *Making vocational choices: A theory of vocational personalities and work environments* (2nd ed.). Englewood Cliffs, NJ: Prentice-Hall.

Holland, J. L. (1994). *Self-Directed Search*. Odessa, FL: Psychological Assessment Resources.

Hoyt, K. B. (1975). *An introduction to career education: A policy paper of the U.S. Office of Education*. Washington, DC: U.S. Office of Education.

Individuals with Disabilities Education Act of 1990, 20 U.S.C. § 1400 et seq.

Jastak, S., & Jastak, G. S. (1987). *Wide Range Interest–Opinion Test*. Wilmington, DE: Jastak Assessment Systems.

Johansson, C. B. (1986). *Career Assessment Inventory*. Minneapolis: National Computer Systems.

Keirsey, D., & Bates, M. (1984). *Please understand me: Character and temperament types*. Del Mar, CA: Prometheus Nemesis Book Co.

Koestler, F. A. (1976). *The unseen minority*. New York: David McKay.

Kokaska, C. J., & Brolin, D. E. (1985). *Career education for handicapped individuals*. Columbus, OH: Charles E. Merrill.

Kraus, L. E., & Stoddard, S. (1989). *Chartbook on disability in the United States*. Washington, DC: National Institute on Disability and Rehabilitation Research.

Kuder, F. (1960). *Kuder Occupational Interest Survey*. Chicago: Science Research Associates.

Louis Harris & Associates. (1986). *The ICD survey of disabled Americans: Bringing disabled Americans into the mainstream*. New York: International Center for the Disabled.

Louis Harris & Associates. (1987). *The ICD survey II: Employing disabled Americans*. New York: International Center for the Disabled.

Louis Harris & Associates. (1989). *The ICD survey III: A report card on special education*. New York: International Center for the Disabled.

Louis Harris & Associates. (1995). *The N.O.D./Harris survey on employment of people with disabilities*. New York: The National Organization on Disability.

Lowenfeld, B. (1973). *The changing status of the blind*. Springfield, IL: Charles C Thomas.

Ludden, L. V. (1992). *Job savvy: How to be a success at work*. Indianapolis, IN: JIST.

Markwardt, F. C. (1989). *Peabody Individual Achievement Test–Revised*. Circle Pines, MN: American Guidance Service.

McCarron, L., & Dial, J. (1986). *McCarron–Dial Evaluation System* (2nd ed.). Dallas, TX: McCarron–Dial Systems.

Mcloughlin, C. S., Garner, J. B., & Callahan, M. (Eds.). (1987). *Getting employed, staying employed: Job development and training for persons with severe handicaps*. Baltimore: Brookes.

McNeil, J. M. (1993). *Americans with disabilities: 1991–1992*. Washington, DC: U.S. Department of Commerce.

Means, B. L., & Roessler, R. T. (1976). *Personal achievement skills*. Fayetteville: Arkansas Rehabilitation Research and Training Center.

Moore, J. E., & Fireison, M. S. (1995). Rehabilitating persons who are blind: 75 years of progress. *American Rehabilitation, 21*(3), 22–27.

National Institute on Disability and Rehabilitation Research. (1994). *Directory of national information sources on disabilities.* Washington, DC: U.S. Office of Special Education and Rehabilitative Services.

National Occupational Information Coordinating Committee. (1986). *Using labor market information in career exploration and decision making.* Garrett Park, MD: Garrett Park Press.

Neff, W. S. (1985). *Work and human behavior* (3rd ed.). New York: Aldine.

Osipow, S. H., & Fitzgerald, L. F. (1996). *Theories of career development* (4th ed.). Boston: Allyn & Bacon.

Parker, R. M., & Szymanski, E. M. (1992). *Rehabilitation counseling: Basics and beyond* (2nd ed.). Austin, TX: PRO-ED.

Parsons, F. (1909). *Choosing a vocation.* Boston: Houghton Mifflin.

Patton, J. R., Kauffman, J. M., Blackbourn, J. M., & Brown, G. B. (1991). *Exceptional children in focus* (5th ed.). New York: Macmillan.

Perry, W. (1970). *Intellectual and ethical development in the college years.* New York: Holt, Rinehart and Winston.

Powell, T. H., Pancsofar, E. L., Steere, D. E., Butterworth, J., Itzkowitz, J. S., & Rainforth, B. (1991). *Supported employment: Providing integrated employment opportunities for persons with disabilities.* New York: Longman.

Power, P. W. (1991). *A guide to vocational assessment.* Austin, TX: PRO-ED.

Raths, L. E., Harmin, M., & Simon, S. B. (1966). *Values and teaching: Working with values in the classroom.* Columbus, OH: Charles E. Merrill.

Rehabilitation Act of 1973, 29 U.S.C. § 701 *et seq.*

Roberts, J. R. (1969). *Pennsylvania Bi-Manual Worksample.* Circle Pines, MN: American Guidance Service.

Roessler, R. T., & Rubin, S. E. (1992). *Case management and rehabilitation counseling: Procedures and techniques.* Austin, TX: PRO-ED.

Rosenberg, P. (1995, November 24). Scope of the AIDS epidemic in the United States. *Science, 270,* 1372–1375.

Rubin, S. E., & Roessler, R. T. (1995). *Foundations of the vocational rehabilitation process.* Austin, TX: PRO-ED.

Rutgers University Staff. (1995). *Mental measurements yearbook.* Highland Park, NJ: Mental Measurements Yearbook Press.

School-to-Work Opportunities Act of 1994, 20 U.S.C. § 2394 *et seq.*

Secretary's Commission on Achieving Necessary Skills. (1991a). *SCANS Blueprint for Action: Building Community Coalitions.* Washington, DC: U.S. Government Printing Office.

Secretary's Commission on Achieving Necessary Skills. (1991b). *What work requires of schools.* Washington, DC: U.S. Government Printing Office.

Secretary's Commission on Achieving Necessary Skills. (1992a). *Learning a Living.* Washington, DC: U.S. Government Printing Office.

Secretary's Commission on Achieving Necessary Skills. (1992b). *Skills and tasks for jobs: A SCANS report for America 2000.* Washington, DC: U.S. Government Printing Office.

Secretary's Commission on Achieving Necessary Skills. (1993). *Teaching the SCANS Competencies.* Washington, DC: U.S. Government Printing Office.

Simon, S. B., Howe, L. W., & Kirschenbaum, H. (1995). *Values clarification.* New York: Warner Books.

Sinetar, M. (1987). *Do what you love, the money will follow.* New York: Dell.

Social Security Act of 1935, 42 U.S.C. § 301 *et seq.*

Spraycar, M. (Ed.). (1995). *Stedman's medical dictionary* (26th ed.). Baltimore: Williams & Wilkins.

Stafford, B. J. (1995). A legislative perspective on the Rehabilitation Act. *American Rehabilitation, 21*(3), 37–42.

Strong, E. K., Campbell, D. P., & Hansen, J. (1985). *The Strong–Campbell Interest Inventory.* Minneapolis: National Computer Systems.

Super, D. E. (1953). A theory of vocational development. *American Psychologist, 8,* 185–190.

Super, D. E. (1976, June). Career education and the meanings of work. *Monographs on Career Education.* U.S. Department of Health, Education and Welfare, U.S. Office of Education.

Super, D. E. (1980). A life-span, life-space approach to career development. *Journal of Vocational Behavior, 13,* 282–298.

Super, D. E. (1990). A life-span, life-space approach to career development. In D. Brown, L. Brooks, & others (Eds.), *Career choice and development* (2nd ed.). San Francisco: Jossey-Bass.

Temelini, D., & Fesko, S. (1997, January). Shared responsibility: Job search practices from the consumer and state vocational rehabilitation perspective. *Research Practice.* Boston: Institute for Community Inclusion.

Texas Employment Commission. (1983). *Qualities employers like, dislike in job applicants: Results of statewide employer survey.* Austin, TX: Author.

Tieger, P. D., & Barron-Tieger, B. (1992). *Do what you are: Discover the perfect career for you through the secrets of personality type*. Boston: Little, Brown.

Tiffin, R. (1948). *Examiner manual for the Purdue Pegboard*. Chicago: Science Research Associates.

U.S. Department of Labor. (1970). *General Aptitude Test Battery*. Washington, DC: U.S. Government Printing Office.

U.S. Department of Labor. (1971). *Non-Reading Aptitude Test Battery*. Washington, DC: U.S. Government Printing Office.

U.S. Department of Labor. (1979). *Guide for occupational exploration*. Washington, DC: U.S. Government Printing Office.

U.S. Department of Labor. (1991). *Dictionary of occupational titles*. Washington, DC: U.S. Government Printing Office.

U.S. Department of Labor. (1996). *Occupational outlook handbook*. Washington, DC: U.S. Government Printing Office.

Wagner, M., D'Amico, R., Marder, C., Newman, L., & Blackorby, J. (1992). *What happens next? Trends in postschool outcomes of youth with disabilities*. Menlo Park, CA: SRI International.

Wechsler, D. (1981). *Wechsler Adult Intelligence Scale–Revised Edition*. San Antonio: Psychological Corporation.

Wegmann, R., Chapman, R., & Johnson, M. (1985). *Looking for work in the new economy*. Salt Lake City: Olympus.

Wehman, P. (1992). *Life beyond the classroom*. Baltimore: Brookes.

Wolffe, K. (1985). Don't give those kids fish! Teach 'em how to fish! *Journal of Visual Impairment and Blindness, 79*(10), 470–472.

Wolffe, K. (1986). The relationship between pre-employment skills training and successful placement of hard-to-employ rehabilitation clients (Doctoral dissertation, University of Texas, 1986). *Dissertation Abstracts International, 47*, 05A.

Wright, G. N. (1980). *Total rehabilitation*. Boston: Little, Brown.

Index

Notes

Notes

Notes

Notes